Snowbird Cherokees

Snowbird Cherokees

✦

People of Persistence

Sharlotte Neely

THE UNIVERSITY OF GEORGIA PRESS

Athens & London

© 1991 by the University of Georgia Press
Athens, Georgia 30602
All rights reserved
Designed by Louise M. Jones
Set in 10½/13 Aldus and Trajanus display
The paper in this book meets the guidelines for
permanence and durability of the Committee on
Production Guidelines for Book Longevity of the
Council on Library Resources.

Printed in the United States of America

95 94 93   C   5 4 3 2

97 96 95   P   5 4 3 2

Library of Congress Cataloging in Publication Data
Neely, Sharlotte, 1948–
Snowbird Cherokees: people of persistence / by Sharlotte Neely.
p.   cm.
Includes bibliographical references (p.   ) and index.
ISBN 0-8203-1327-0 (alk. paper)
ISBN 0-8203-1575-3 (pbk.: alk. paper)
1. Cherokee Indians—Social life and customs.
2. North Carolina—Social life and customs.
I. Title.
E99.C5N44   1991
975.6'004975—dc20
90-11308   CIP

British Library Cataloging in Publication Data available

This book is dedicated with gratitude to my parents,
Kathleen and Joe Neely,
and to my husband and daughter,
Tom and Bridgette Donnelly

Contents

◄◄◄◄◄◄◄ ◄◆► ►►►►►►►

Acknowledgments

Many people deserve thanks for their assistance in this undertaking. Those who merit the greatest appreciation are the Snowbird Cherokees themselves, who are the living embodiment of the Harmony Ethic. Snowbird people were more generous with me than they could often afford to be. They took great time answering my questions, letting me stay with them, and allowing me to be part of their lives. Snowbird is a community of love and sharing. I am especially grateful to the descendants of the late Gaffney and Susie Long: Ned and Shirley Long and their children, Patricia, Johnny, Ned, Jr., and Brenda, and grandchildren and Ella Jackson and the late Ed Jackson and their children, William, Lou Ellen, Gilliam, Jacob, Shirley, Ethel, and Esther, and grandchildren, who let me be a part of their families.

I am also grateful to the Eastern Band of Cherokees as a whole and to the Museum of the Cherokee Indian, especially archivist Joan Greene Orr. While every Cherokee I have met has been concerned and helpful about my research, only I should be held responsible for any errors and the theoretical interpretations presented here.

A great deal of gratitude goes to the late John J. Honigmann of the University of North Carolina. I value his insight and advice as a mentor, Amerindianist, anthropologist, and friend. Irma Honigmann also provided emotional support. Special thanks go as well to Cherokee expert John Gulick. His book, *Cherokees at the Crossroads*, inspired me to do fieldwork with the Cherokees. I am honored that he chose me to write the epilogue to the second edition of *Crossroads*. Other teachers who have helped shape the points of view contained in this work include Richard A. Yarnell, Terence M. S. Evens, Robert E. Daniels, Dorothea C. Leighton, Joffre L. Coe, Meridith Jean Black, Lewis H. Larson, and the late Henry T. Malone. For their help in my academic development as an Amerindianist, I would also like to thank Theda Perdue, Alfonso Ortiz, Harriet J. Kupferer, Wendell H. Oswalt, Raymond D. Fogelson, Nancy O. Lurie, James A. Clifton, Burton L. Purrington, Duane H. King, William Cook, J. Anthony Paredes, John H. Peterson, Charles M. Hudson, Harry A. Kersey, William McKee Evans, and Helen C. Rountree. Though I have never met him, I continue to be inspired by the writings of Norwegian anthropologist Fredrik Barth.

My colleagues at Northern Kentucky University are the kind who support research and publication, and I am grateful to them for that attitude. I would like to thank in particular three individuals who have encouraged the writing and rewriting of this particular endeavor: anthropologists Christopher Boehm and James F. Hopgood and sociologist Lyle A. Gray. NKU geographer Ray Rappold drew all the maps.

The secretarial staff at NKU, under the leadership of Jean Featherstone, are the best, and I would like to single out for thanks Darlene Stroberg, a student of Indian culture who typed the final draft of *Snowbird Cherokees.*

My thanks also go to everyone in my home state at the University of Georgia Press, especially Malcolm L. Call, Madelaine Cooke, Nancy Grayson Holmes, and Louise M. Jones, and to freelance copyeditor Loris Mann. I am also grateful to photographer Kenneth Murray from Kingsport, Tennessee.

I must specifically thank my family for their emotional, spiritual, intellectual, and financial support, especially my mother M. Kathleen Bell Neely of Atlanta, Georgia, and my late father, Joseph Bowden Neely, my first and most important teachers, who steadfastly encouraged me in my education, career, and writing. My father died of a heart attack on November 19, 1974, and Snowbird Cherokee friends he and my mother had made through me attended his funeral. Some months before, he had assisted the Snowbird Rescue Squad in procuring a badly needed ambulance. It was a great comfort to me upon losing my father to have my Cherokee "family" there for support.

Finally, I would like to express my gratitude to my husband, attorney and fellow anthropologist, Thomas Christian Donnelly, for his encouragement, ideas, faith in my abilities, and enthusiastic support of my career and writing. I hope the two of us can give our daughter, Mary Kathleen Bridgette Donnelly, the kind of support my parents gave me.

Snowbird Cherokees

◄◄◄◄◄◄◄ ◄◄◊► ►►►►►►►

Introduction

Overleaf: A mist hangs over Graham County's Snowbird Creek, which cuts through the mountainous reservation lands of the Snowbird Cherokees.
Photo by Ken Murray, 1990.

WHEN I FIRST BECAME AWARE of the North Carolina Snowbird Cherokee community and began developing a framework for the study of the
group's position in contemporary American society, I assumed that the
bulk of my research would focus on the interethnic aspect of ethnic
relations, between Indians and local whites. In research and later in writing, however, I devoted an equal amount or more time to intraethnic
relations, both between the isolated Snowbird community itself and the
other Eastern Cherokee communities on the main reservation and between Eastern (North Carolina) and Western (Oklahoma) Cherokees as
a whole. No matter whether the focus was interethnic or intraethnic
relations, my overriding point of view became adaptive strategies.

Snowbird proved in many ways to be an ideal community for such
a study. The group may be the most traditionalist of North Carolina
Cherokee communities, and yet it has purposely cultivated close ties
with both local whites and Oklahoma Cherokees. Located fifty miles
from the main reservation, Snowbird has been isolated from many of
the problems other North Carolina Cherokees have experienced. Add to
this the fact that this is the first study of the Snowbird Cherokees and
it should become apparent that not only can new ground be explored
but many of the "givens" we assume about the Cherokees have to be
re-examined.

One given in particular has to be re-examined in light of the Snowbird Cherokees. Snowbird, interestingly, is both the most traditionalist
Cherokee community and the Cherokee community with the most intense, long-term relations with local whites. In examining this seeming
paradox, one comes to the conclusion that in the last century, since the
creation of the Eastern Cherokee reservation, "white Indians" have been
more of a threat to traditionalism than whites have. For most of the last
one hundred years, Snowbird has had less contact with white Indians
than any other Cherokee community. It therefore became necessary to
examine the effects of both interethnic and intraethnic relations. Such
an examination will reveal the reasons for the above conclusion.

There are several reasons for focusing on an intraethnic dimension in
such a study. One reason relates to the original purpose of the research,
which was to focus on Indian-white relations. Since many subgroupings
within the Eastern Band are perceived as divisions along a red-white continuum (from fullbloods to white Indians to "wanna-bees" to whites),
dealing with all Eastern Cherokees as a single group versus whites does

not fully explain the situation. In their own racial-cultural terms, the Eastern Band of Cherokee Indians do not perceive of themselves as a homogeneous group. It is therefore necessary to deal with the intra-ethnic as well as the interethnic situation in order to explain adequately ethnic relations in general.

In addition, political factionalism within Native American communities, or intraethnic relations, has been dealt with only minimally by anthropologists. Snowbird Cherokee Gilliam Jackson writes: "Today there is a great deal of factionalism, a lot of which is due to our gradual assimilation into the dominant society."[1] Factionalism is a subject worthy of more attention. The famous 1973 episode at Wounded Knee, South Dakota, to name but the most obvious example, demonstrates how little political factionalism is understood for a group like the Pine Ridge Sioux. One aspect of intraethnic relations considered here deals with factionalism among the Eastern Cherokees.

It is also unfortunate that most studies of subgroupings within Native American groups focus almost exclusively on behavioral typologies. The Cherokees themselves have been categorized as Conservative, Generalized, "Rural-white," and Middle-Class Indian. Much of this kind of psychological anthropology is of a high quality. The problem is that typologies other than behavioral ones have not been compiled by researchers. Behavioral categorizations of Indian communities have almost always been developed by outsiders and are rarely the primary basis upon which tribal members classify each other. An insider's perspective reveals broader, less concise, working categories with which people actually operate. In order to analyze political factionalism, for example, power-group categories become more important than behavioral ones.

There are also reasons for studying intertribal relations between Eastern and Western Cherokees. Unlike many western tribes, Native Americans in the eastern United States are sometimes viewed as if they were not really Indians. Often these groups, while dealing frequently with non-Indians, rarely deal with Indians other than those from their own tribe. These eastern groups are considered isolated, not only physically but culturally, from other Native Americans. Recently intensified relations between Eastern and Western Cherokees demonstrate that groups do make serious efforts to overcome physical isolation and in the process reduce much of their cultural isolation. An examination here of a religious ceremony in which Eastern and Western Cherokees participate demonstrates such an effort. It also demonstrates that fullbloods and Cherokee-language speakers, whether from Oklahoma or North Carolina, often perceive of themselves as more closely related to each other than to white Indians within their own groups.

Of course, this undertaking also deals with interethnic relations between Cherokee Indians and whites. It focuses on the successful (from the Cherokees' point of view) rather than the unsuccessful or exploitative side of those relations. Native Americans are often portrayed in the popular literature as being ineffectual in dealing with whites, and this stereotype is used as a justification for not removing paternalistic and discriminatory policies. The small Snowbird Cherokee community is among Indian groups who are reasonably successful in their dealings with whites, and this is the type of situation which is described here.

There are several points of view not covered in depth in this research which could be profitably undertaken by someone in the future. This study views ethnic relations from the perspective of a small fullblood community. There is, however, also the small white Indian community of Tomotla in Cherokee County, North Carolina, which has never been the subject of scholarly inquiry. Ethnic relations from that community's perspective are probably quite different. Intertribal relations between the two Cherokee groups as viewed from Oklahoma, rather than North Carolina, should also be a profitable future study. In addition, it seems that Indian-white relations when studied by anthropologists are almost always viewed from the Indian community's perspective. More studies of the reverse should be useful and especially interesting if the research were undertaken by an Indian anthropologist.

Finally, in the following chapters several phrases are used which should be defined in order to understand the tribe or community being referred to at any one time. The term "non-Indians" almost always means whites, since blacks and other ethnic groups are not numerous in the southern Appalachians. "Non-Indians" is used rather than "whites" because "non-Indians" is the term Cherokees use. "North Carolina Cherokees," "Eastern Band of Cherokee Indians," "EBCI," "Eastern Cherokees," or simply "Eastern Band" are synonymous. "Oklahoma Cherokees" are often also referred to as "Western Cherokees." In North Carolina the "main reservation" is the "Qualla Boundary," which to Indians living elsewhere is simply "Cherokee." Of the five political townships (Big Cove, Wolfetown, Birdtown, Painttown, and Yellow Hill) located on the

Qualla Boundary, however, Yellow Hill alone is sometimes referred to as "Cherokee" by Qualla Boundary residents. To confuse the matter further, some townships have more than one recognized community, each with a different name. The main divisions of Wolfetown are "Soco" and "Big 'Y'," while Birdtown is divided into "Birdtown proper" and the "Thirty-two Hundred Acre Tract" ("the Thomas Tract"). The sixth township, not located on the Qualla Boundary, is "Cheoah," which is the subject of the political controversy described in a following chapter. The traditionalist Cherokees of Snowbird in Graham County assert that Cheoah and Snowbird are synonymous, while the white Indians of Tomotla in Cherokee County claim they also are part of Cheoah. Particularly confusing is the term "Cherokee" which can refer to the Eastern or Western Bands, or both, a North Carolina county, Yellow Hill township, the Qualla Boundary, or even a language. References to the maps should help diminish confusion over geographical terms.

Two other terms should also be clarified, "white Indians" and "fullbloods" (or "real Indians"). These terms are not precise scholarly terms but phrases commonly used among North Carolina's Cherokee population. In *Cherokees at the Crossroads*, the most complete study of the Eastern Cherokees in the modern era, John Gulick explains that as behavioral terms white Indian and fullblood represent a false dichotomy. Yet Gulick goes on to say that: "It [the dichotomy] exists in the heads of the Eastern Cherokees and to such a degree that it is a theme to which informants revert over and over again."[2]

Although the terms have a racial connotation, and this is one of the meanings attached to them by many Cherokees, they are used here as intraethnic labels in an effort to explain a cultural, not a racial, situation. The terms are used by both groups of Cherokees to refer to each other and themselves. White Indian does not necessarily refer to those phenotypically white, just as fullblood may mean someone of nearly total, but not exclusive, Cherokee blood degree. When pressed, most Cherokees will explain that a fullblood, or real Indian, is someone who "acts Indian," while a white Indian "acts white." Gulick further explains:

> "Full-Blood" implies 100 per cent Indian inheritance, and yet we discovered many instances of "Full-Bloods" who had less than ¼ Indian inheritance and even some rare instances of "Full-Bloods" who were not particularly Indian in physical appearance. While there was a general concentration of

"Full-Bloods" in the ¾–⁴⁄₄ range, there were enough exceptions to indicate that other criteria besides sheer inheritance enter into the definition. The same problem arose in regards to "White Indians." . . . There appeared to be no middle ground and there definitely is no middle ground as far as the labels are concerned.[3]

It should be noted that as of the mid-1970s, 75.5 percent of Snowbird's adult population, even counting intermarried non-Indians, were legally "fullblood Cherokees," and 80.5 percent were legally within the three-fourths to fullblood range. If intermarried non-Cherokees are not considered part of the community, 91.4 percent of Snowbird's adults were within the three-fourths to fullblood range. During the 1956–57 academic year when Gulick analyzed the blood degree of students in reservation schools, he found that 96 percent of Snowbird's students were biological fullbloods, a greater percentage than in any other Cherokee community, including traditionalist Big Cove with 31 percent fullbloods.[4] While the percentage of fullbloods in Snowbird dropped from the 1950s to the 1970s and continues to drop in the 1990s as intermarriage with whites increases, Snowbird still has a larger percentage of fullbloods than any other Eastern Cherokee community. It is also important to note that the fullblood–white Indian dichotomy is not uniquely Cherokee but exists in many, if not most, Native American communities.

The main method here in analyzing ethnic relations, as viewed from the Snowbird Cherokee community, consists of situational analysis, or the extended-case method. The method and its application are described more fully in a later chapter. Preceding that chapter is one that provides geographical, historical, and cultural background, and another on ethnic relations. After those two chapters come two that describe situations to which the extended-case method is applied: a political controversy that illuminates intraethnic relations among the Eastern Cherokees and a ceremony that describes interethnic relations between Indians and whites and intertribal relations between Eastern and Western Cherokees. A concluding chapter re-examines Snowbird ethnic relations in general in a theoretical context.

The focus throughout is on cultural persistence, rather than acculturation. This is a unique way of viewing a Cherokee community. As historian John R. Finger has pointed out: "Cherokee 'progress' supplemented Cherokee treaty rights as an argument against enforced removal. . . .

During the next 150 years historians and popular writers alike conjured up a compelling stereotype—the 'civilized' Cherokee. . . . Today, however, one might safely question the extent of tribal civilization. . . . But what usually impresses Americans is change rather than continuity."[5]

This is a study of continuity.

1

Land of the Sky People

Overleaf: The Thunderbird area is typical of the environment that
has sheltered the Snowbird Cherokees for thousands of years.
Man-made lakes now dot the countryside.
Photo by Ken Murray, 1990.

A series of mountains rise out of the great Appalachian Range in Graham County, North Carolina, southwest of the Great Smoky Mountains. For my people, the Eastern Band of Cherokees, it is an old, old landmark and they gave it the name Snowbird Mountains because it is said that long ago there once lived on the highest peak a giant white snowbird who was the grandfather of all the little snowbirds we see today.

To me, this region is the top of the whole world—the land of the Sky People, it was said. The skyline is in all directions and close at hand. It is a land of cold, rushing rivers, small creeks, deep gorges, dark timber, and waterfalls. Great billowing clouds sail upon the mountains and in early morning a blue-gray mist hangs just above the treetops.[1]

THUS, THE INDIAN AUTHOR, TRAVELLER BIRD, describes Snowbird, his Cherokee grandfather's home. Boxed in by the Snowbird, Unicoi, Yellow, and Cheoah Mountains of Graham County in the southern Appalachians, the landscape of the isolated Snowbird community differs markedly from that of other Cherokee communities to the northeast. The main reservation, Cherokee, is littered with the enterprises of tourism while Snowbird still has much of the pristine quality which Traveller Bird describes.

The Cherokees may be the most studied Native Americans in North America. They have attracted the attention of numerous anthropologists as well as social scientists, including historians and sociologists, from fields that do not typically study Indians. The Cherokees have been studied in both their North Carolina and Oklahoma homes, and they have been studied as they existed both before and after the removal. But somehow Snowbird had never been the focus of any study. When I "discovered" Snowbird, almost by accident on a trip that took place to observe education on the Qualla Boundary, I knew I had found the place of my first fieldwork.

As I drove along Snowbird Creek, I saw dark forests, old Indian cabins interspersed with modern homes under construction, and the Snowbird Cherokees themselves. Here walking along the road was an elderly woman with her hair in the traditional red kerchief and wearing an

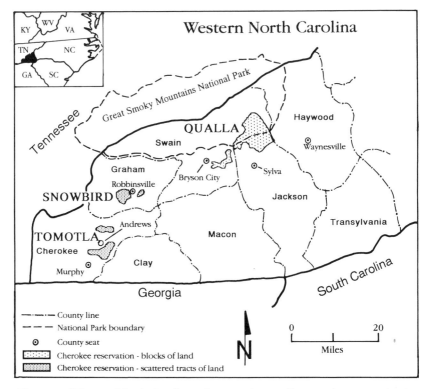

Figure 1. Western North Carolina, showing the Qualla Boundary, Snowbird, and Tomotla reservation lands

Indian corn-bead necklace. There was a teenage boy with jeans and a T-shirt. Both looked fullblood. Two years later I approached Ned Long and other members of the community about doing fieldwork there. Indian communities are some of the few places where people know exactly what it is that anthropologists do. So when I described my goal to study Snowbird, Ned said something to the effect of, "It's about time. All the other anthropologists have worked up in Cherokee. We'll show you how 'real Indians' live."

SNOWBIRD'S UNIQUENESS

Snowbird is different from other Eastern Cherokee communities, and the absence of tourism is only one way in which Snowbird is different.

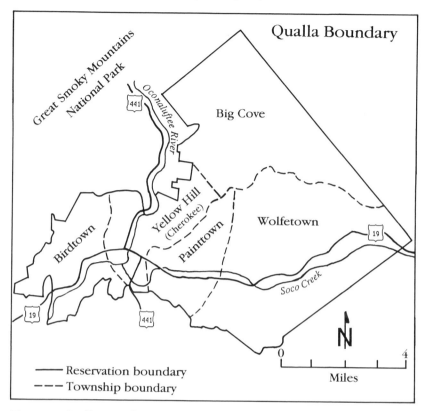

Figure 2. Qualla Boundary, showing the five townships on the main reservation

Most studies of the Eastern Band have focused upon the traditionalist Big Cove community on the Qualla Boundary.[2] Yet, Snowbird has a higher percentage of both fullbloods and Cherokee-language speakers than Big Cove or any other Eastern Cherokee community, and for the Cherokees themselves these two characteristics seem to be the most important criteria for judging how traditional an individual or a community is.[3] Like Big Cove, Snowbird is considered a "real Indian" community. Snowbird has other traditional characteristics, too: for example, a high percentage of native craftsmen and some Indian doctors with a knowledge of medicinal plants.[4]

In addition to being perhaps the most traditional community among the Eastern Cherokees, Snowbird is unique in other ways. Its reservation

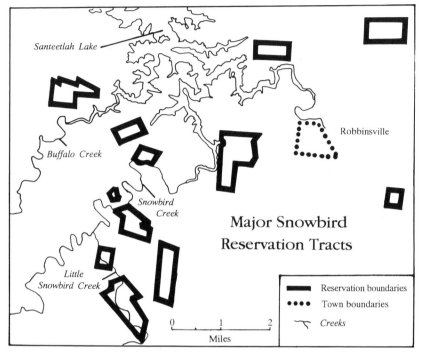

Figure 3. Major Snowbird reservation tracts in Graham County

lands are scattered into individual tracts of land along Snowbird, Little Snowbird, and Buffalo creeks, not consolidated into a huge land mass like the Qualla Boundary. The way Snowbird reservation lands are inter-mingled with white-owned lands has resulted in the inability of Snow-bird Cherokees to withdraw physically from the larger white American world. At the same time, the location of Snowbird lands more than fifty miles from the Qualla Boundary has imposed a kind of isolation from other Eastern Cherokees.

How does a community, like Snowbird, remain intensely traditional while both removed from other Indian communities and located in such close proximity to white communities? Moreover, how does a tradition-alist community, like Snowbird, become skilled at adapting to the larger political and economic world without losing its traditionalism? In order to answer these types of questions, anthropologist James Mooney first called for a study of Snowbird in the 1880s. This work, one hundred years later, is the first and only response to Mooney's call.

ABORIGINAL CULTURE

The Snowbird Cherokee Indian population of Graham County, about 380 people in 1980, has ancient origins, as does the rest of the Eastern Cherokee population. The Cherokees have probably been native to the southern Appalachians for at least four thousand years. By the beginning of the historic period, the Cherokees numbered more than twenty thousand making them one of the largest Indian nations in North America north of Mexico. They lived on land or held hunting territory in nine modern states: Alabama, Georgia, Tennessee, Kentucky, Mississippi, the Carolinas, and the Virginias. The mountain and hill country offered varied resources for subsistence, and the Cherokees, through cultivation of corn, beans, squash, pumpkins, and other crops, as well as gathering, fishing, and hunting, achieved a highly successful generalized adaptation.

During the early part of the historic period approximately eighty towns of twelve to two hundred households each were dispersed throughout five regions. The Middle and Out settlements of central western North Carolina spoke the Kituhwa dialect of Cherokee, which is still spoken on the Qualla Boundary. The Valley settlements of southwestern North Carolina and the Overhill settlements of eastern Tennessee spoke the Atali dialect, variations of which are still spoken in the Snowbird community and in Oklahoma. The Lower settlements of South Carolina and Georgia spoke the Elati dialect, which is now extinct. The Cherokee language is part of the Iroquoian language family.

In an aboriginal Cherokee town, sweathouses, gardens, and rectangular, gabled, wattle-and-daub homes clustered around a square ground. On the west side of the square ground stood a council house, legendarily seven-sided, on a small temple mound. If the town were on the fringes of the Cherokee territory, it was probably surrounded by a stockade as protection from enemy warriors.

The household was the basic unit of Cherokee social organization. As was typical of southeastern Indians, residence was matrilocal; thus a newly married couple lived with the wife's family. Legendarily there had always been seven matrilineal clans: the Deer, Wolf, Bird, Wild Potato, Red Paint, Blue Plant, and Long Hair or Twister. From the individual's perspective, four of the clans were most important: one's own (which was also one's mother's and maternal grandmother's), one's father's (which was also one's paternal grandmother's), and each of one's grandfathers'. Individuals were prohibited from marrying into the first two clans and encouraged to marry into either the maternal grandfather's clan or paternal grandfather's clan. The Cherokees used a variation on a Crow kinship terminology. While many people today on the main reservation are not aware of their clan affiliation, most Snowbird Cherokees are.

The aboriginal Cherokee political system was a chiefdom based on the dichotomy between the peace and war factions, with the peace faction dominant. The peace faction, composed mostly of older men, represented the civil and religious leadership. There was one principal chief, the Uku, for the entire nation. He had seven assistants, including a right-hand man, a speaker, and five other advisers, as well as a group of minor officials, some of whom were priests and shamans. The war faction, composed mostly of younger men, represented the military leadership. The principal war chief was assisted by three main officers, seven counselors, and the war woman, a young Cherokee female of exceptional courage, who participated in the decision-making.

Cherokee religious and ceremonial life centered around seven festivals, many of them reflecting the interest in the annual cycle of farming. One of these festivals, the Green Corn Ceremony, persisted into the early twentieth century. Seven was a magic number to the Cherokees as evidenced by their seven ceremonies, seven clans, seven-sided council houses, and the seven directions (north, south, east, west, up, down, and here).

PRE-REMOVAL AND REMOVAL HISTORY

By the eighteenth century, however, direct warfare against whites; intertribal warfare, caused by the pressure for land as white settlers pushed inland; and diseases, mostly smallpox, had all begun to decimate the Cherokee population. In times of warfare the Cherokees may have fled from the bottomlands, where they largely lived and farmed, up into the more mountainous areas for refuge; the Snowbird region of Graham County may have served as one of those refuge areas.

Diseases and warfare continued into the nineteenth century, and a new threat emerged as well: removal. The early years of the nineteenth century saw the beginning of intense efforts by whites and by some factions of Cherokees to change Cherokee culture. White efforts at culture change centered in the more accessible hill country of northern Georgia, northeastern Alabama, eastern Tennessee, and extreme southern North Carolina. Traders, missionaries, and church-affiliated educators streamed into the area. White-Indian intermarriage increased, and, as a result, by the 1830s many prominent Cherokee leaders were white Indians. Matrilineal descent among the Cherokees made the offspring of white male–Cherokee female unions full members of Cherokee society no matter what their blood degree or in what cultural tradition they had been raised. Even the United States government recognized all whites who had intermarried with Cherokees or been adopted by them before 1836 (the year the Cherokee Nation "legally" ceased to exist as a result of the ratification of the Treaty of New Echota) as Cherokee Indians and enrolled them on the Henderson Roll of 1835.[5] The federal government, in effect, sanctioned the addition of non-Indians into Cherokee society. If approved by Tribal Council, blacks could also be enumerated as Cherokees.

The factionalism that exists today between real Indians and white Indians can be traced back to the nineteenth century when these factions then had a geographical correspondence; most white Indians lived to the south in the hill country while most fullbloods lived to the north in the mountains. The racial terms, fullblood and white Indian, also carried cultural connotations in that the term fullblood represented cultural traditionalism while white Indian was associated with acculturation. Fullbloods, or conservatives, rarely came into contact with white traders, missionaries, and educators while white Indians, or progressives, often did, and white Indians frequently had whites as kinsmen by blood or by marriage.

In North Carolina it is possible to draw a line separating pre-removal northern Cherokee conservatives from southern Cherokee progressives. Such a boundary can be established at the Snowbird Mountains. To the southeast of these mountains, at what is now the town of Andrews in Cherokee County, were the northernmost permanent, pre-removal missions and schools: the Valleytown Baptist and Methodist missions.[6] Northwest of these mountains and continuing up into the Smokey Mountains were the homes of Cherokee conservatives. Here were included the towns of Kituhwa, near present-day Cherokee on the Qualla Boundary in Swain County; and Cheoah, near the site of what is now Robbinsville, the county seat of Graham County, where today's Snowbird Cherokee community is located. Apparently, an effort was made around 1817 to found a mission in this northern area, but, if established at all, it did not last for long.

In the southern hill country, the early nineteenth century was a period of rapid cultural transformation. The Cherokees there attempted to remodel Cherokee society after that of white Americans. A constitution, patterned after the United States' version, was written which provided for executive, legislative, and judicial branches of government. The Cherokee Nation was divided into eight districts (Aquohee, Amohee, Chattooga, Chickamauga, Cossawattee, Etowah, Hickory Log, and Taquohee), each sending representatives to the two houses of government at the newly established capital of New Echota, near present-day Calhoun, in Gordon County, Georgia. Buildings at New Echota were patterned after American architectural styles, and both a white missionary, Samuel Worchester, and the Indian newspaper editor of the *Cherokee Phoenix*, Elias Boudinot, had houses built in a distinctively New England style. Near New Echota at Spring Place, in Murray County, Georgia, stood the columned antebellum mansion of the white Indian Vann family, slave-owners who operated a plantation.

Some techno-economic changes probably filtered into the conservative communities in the mountains very early in the form of new crops, livestock, tools, and guns, but few social or religious changes seem to have a pre-removal date there. By the 1820s for example, Cherokees in North Carolina were herding sheep and cattle, although they were still not engaged in completely American-style farming endeavors.

Geographer Douglas C. Wilms has compiled statistics on pre-removal slave-owning among the Cherokees, figures that show a marked contrast in acculturation by both faction and region. The Cherokee Census of 1835, the Henderson Roll, shows that there were only 37 slaves owned by North Carolina Cherokees, whereas 1,553 slaves were owned by Cherokees in other areas: in Georgia, 776; Tennessee, 480; and Alabama, 297.[7] Of those 37 slaves in North Carolina, only 12 were owned by fullblood families while 25, or about twice as many, were owned by white Indians. Most white Indian families and more than one-third of all families with an intermarried white resident were slave-owners while only 10 percent of fullbloods owned slaves. In addition, slaves owned by fullbloods numbered only 4 percent of the total slave population, showing that even among fullbloods who owned slaves there were no large slave-operated plantations. These statistics demonstrate to what degree the Cherokees of the southern hill country had been assimilated into the local white American economy, in contrast to the Cherokees of the mountains, who were pursuing much more traditional economic patterns.

The pre-removal North Carolina Cherokees are frequently described as conservatives. John R. Finger asserts that "beneath the upper socio-economic level was a surprisingly durable stratum of traditionalism, especially in North Carolina." James Mooney traces the widening of the gap between conservatives and progressives to the period immediately after the Revolutionary War, and Henry M. Owl, an Eastern Cherokee writing in the 1920s, says that by the time of the removal the Cherokees in the mountains were still "the purest-blooded and most conservative."[8] Marion Starkey describes the difference between the hill country area and the mountains: "The land of greatest fertility lay in northwest Georgia along the headwaters of the tobacco-colored Coosa and the Savannah, and in northeastern Alabama. . . . At least half the Cherokee population was centered in the rolling upland country of up-state Georgia. . . . Along the Tennessee-North Carolina borders, where the mountains are at their most rugged, one entered into the wildest part of the Nation. . . . Here there were no plantations or great houses; tribal customs were most tenacious and least diluted here."[9]

The "wildest part of the Nation" comprised the Aquohee District that included the town of Cheoah, or Buffalo, from which the present-day Snowbird Cherokee community of Graham County, North Carolina, traces its origins. Beyond the boundaries of the Cherokee Nation were the Oconaluftee Indians of North Carolina, ancestors of today's Qualla Boundary Cherokees, who lived on land ceded to the United States in 1819. Like the Cherokees within the Aquohee District, those living near its borders were cultural conservatives and largely fullbloods.

When removal became a reality in the spring of 1838, it is ironic that most of the acculturated white Indian population, some sixteen thousand people, was removed, while most of those Cherokees who remained were fullbloods and conservatives. In 1848 the Mullay Roll described the traditionalist North Carolina post-removal population as "a moral and comparatively industrious people—sober and orderly to a marked degree—and although almost wholly ignorant of our language (not a single full-blood and but a few of the half-breeds speaking English) advancing encouragingly in the acquirement of a knowledge of agriculture, the ordinary mechanical branches, and in spinning, weaving, etc."[10]

The irony is that many white Indian Cherokee leaders had assumed that, as a strategy, adapting completely to white-American lifestyles would demonstrate that the Cherokees were worthy neighbors, not dangerous savages, and therefore not candidates for removal. Whether or not the Cherokees were acculturating was, however, hardly a factor in the removal question. The basic reasons for the Cherokee removal were economic and environmental. The hill country where white Indian progressives dominated was fertile for farming and rich in gold; the mountains where fullblood conservatives lived were deficient both in gold and bottomlands for farming. In the Georgia hill country where whites pushed harder for valuable Cherokee lands, the Indians were removed. In North Carolina fewer demands for Indian lands meant less pressure for the Indians to be removed.

The proof that the North Carolina Cherokees escaped removal for economic and environmental reasons can be demonstrated by looking at other southeastern Indians who also escaped the white onslaught on their lands. Brewton Berry, William H. Gilbert, Edward T. Price, and others have shown that there is a direct correlation between the survival of Indians in the southeast and the poor quality of the land on which they have been allowed to remain.[11] Many surviving Indians, whether on reservations or not, are located on marginal lands, such as the swamps of the Seminoles or the mountains of the Cherokees. Today those southeastern Indian groups with the largest amount of land are also those who possess the poorest quality land.

Even within the southern Appalachians, Cherokee land has less bottomlands than the land of the Cherokees' closest white neighbors, and Snowbird Cherokee lands are among the most mountainous on the reservation and in the region.[12] The removal-era traditionalist chief of some of the North Carolina Cherokees, Yonaguska, clearly realized at the time of removal that his group might remain in the east due to the marginal nature of their land. The late-nineteenth-century anthropologist, James Mooney, having interviewed people who knew Yonaguska, concluded: "Although frequent pressure was brought to bear to induce him and his people to remove to the West, he firmly resisted every persuasion, declaring that the Indians were safer from aggression among their rocks and mountains than they could ever be in a land which the white man could find profitable, and that the Cherokee could be happy only in the country where nature had planted him."[13]

There were, of course, other than strictly environmental and economic causes for the survival of Cherokees in North Carolina. Apparently North Carolina Cherokees were united in their opposition to removal. This was true whether the Cherokees were within the 1830s boundaries of the Cherokee Nation (Graham and Cherokee County settlements) or beyond (Chief Yonaguska's Oconaluftee Indians of the Swain and Jackson County areas). Finger suggests: "Yonaguska . . . had argued against moving. If they did, he said, the government would soon want their new lands, too. There was no limit to white greed."[14] Thus, the North Carolina Cherokees were determined in their convictions not to be removed.

In the summer of 1832 some three thousand gold hunters from Georgia, where the gold rush had begun in 1828, spilled over into North Carolina where they were pushed out again, not only by federal troops but by the "Light-Horse," a mounted Cherokee guard. Although some of the gold hunters did manage to set up camp along the Valley River in the Cherokee County area, "They did not molest the Cheoih [Cheoah] gold mines some distance to the north" in the Graham County, or Snowbird, area.[15] Resorting to a show of force, in the form of the "Light-Horse," further demonstrates the North Carolina Cherokees' conviction not to allow whites to push them off their lands.

A similar resolve also existed among many Georgia Cherokees, but, unfortunately, did not help them to persist. Mary Young describes that conviction on the part of the Cherokees not to be removed: "When General Winfield Scott and several thousand eager but quarrelsome volunteers from the surrounding states arrived in May of 1838, bayonets gleaming and resolve intact, they found freshly-split fence-rails and half-built barns testifying to the Cherokee conviction that the land was still theirs."[16]

White Georgians had pushed hard for the removal of the Cherokees, and the image persists of President Andrew Jackson defying the United States Supreme Court and moving ahead with removal. In 1838, under President Martin Van Buren, United States soldiers and state militiamen implemented the provisions of the fraudulent Treaty of New Echota and rounded up Cherokees into concentration camps all through the summer and fall. Over the winter of 1838–39 they marched them west to Indian

Territory, now Oklahoma. Of about sixteen thousand people, between one-fourth and one-half died on the "Trail of Tears" from either diseases, exposure, malnutrition, or outright murder. Most of the victims were children. About one thousand individuals remained in the east, mostly in the mountains of North Carolina, as the nucleus of today's Snowbird and Qualla Boundary Cherokees.

Economic and environmental situations, coupled with state policies arising out of those situations, must then be singled out as the primary cause for the persistence of Cherokees in North Carolina. North Carolina had previously acquired some Cherokee lands by treaty, and those lands left were not that valuable. Since there were few demands for a land lottery in North Carolina, the state sold its Cherokee lands and found buyers in the people who valued the land most: the Cherokees. One such group of buyers were the Cherokees in the Snowbird area of Graham County who, within mere weeks of removal, purchased over twelve hundred acres of land in the names of three white men, since Indians in North Carolina could not legally own land until after the Civil War. The Cherokee Census of 1835 shows 484 Indians living in the town of Cheoah (Snowbird) and 77 living in Stecoah, both within the Graham County area.[17] There are now about 380 Cherokees and 2,249 acres of scattered Cherokee land in Graham County.[18]

Technically, those Cherokees in the Graham and Cherokee County areas were all doomed to removal since they were legally within the boundaries of the Cherokee Nation and, therefore, subject to the 1835 removal Treaty of New Echota. Many escaped removal by fleeing into the mountains as refugees, as did Euchella's and Tsali's bands, but current oral tradition notwithstanding, many of the Cherokees who remained in the east, specifically the Oconaluftee Indians, did not accomplish this by a mass flight into the mountains. Others, such as some of those in the Graham County area, purchased from North Carolina the land from which they would have been removed. Although Indians, and other non-whites, were then unable legally to own land in North Carolina, these purchases could be made in the names of friendly whites, such as William Holland Thomas, adopted son of Chief Yonaguska, local trader, tribal attorney, fluent Cherokee-language speaker, and, upon Yonaguska's death, "white chief of the Cherokees."[19]

A large number of North Carolina Cherokees were never serious candidates for removal. These were the "Oconaluftee," or "Quallatown,"

Indians of the Swain and Jackson County areas which now comprise the main Cherokee reservation, the Qualla Boundary. When the land that the Qualla Boundary is now on was ceded by the Cherokees to the United States in 1819, at least 50 families of about 393 people never moved from the ceded territory to lands within the Cherokee Nation.[20] Instead they relinquished their Cherokee status and became citizens of North Carolina, a new status which legally protected them from removal. If their land had been valuable enough, however, it is doubtful that even their citizenship could have rescued them from removal.

The *Friends' Weekly Intelligencer* described the process by which the Oconaluftee Indians became North Carolina citizens: "No law of the United States forbidding such a course, and North Carolina giving full assent . . . and inviting not only the half-blood Cherokees, but the full-blood Indians, who chose to remain in the land of their fathers, to take protection under the aegis of her laws, nothing more was necessary to make them citizens, but a continued residence within her limits twelve months agreeably to the laws of the state." The petition of the Oconaluftee Indians to become North Carolina citizens had been accompanied by certificates from local whites describing the Cherokees as "a sober, temperate, and industrious people, improving in civilization, the knowledge of the arts, and agriculture; and that they were qualified to make useful citizens."[21] Although legal status as state citizens aided some North Carolina Cherokees in remaining east, even a Supreme Court decision in their favor had not saved the Cherokees in Georgia from being removed from their valuable lands there.

POST-REMOVAL HISTORY

After the removal of 1838 almost all the thousand Cherokees left in the east were within western North Carolina. Technological and social changes filtered into the area with some rapidity, and Cherokee men replaced women in the traditional role as farmers. Christianity also spread quickly, although Indian, not white, ministers were the rule. A traveler, Charles Lanman, passed through the North Carolina Cherokee region in 1848 and described the change in Cherokee culture:

> They manufacture their own clothing, their own ploughs, and other farm-ing utensils, their own axes, and even their own guns. . . . They keep the

same domestic animals that are kept by their white neighbors, and cultivate all the common grains of the country. . . . They are chiefly Methodists and Baptists. . . . They have their own courts and try their criminals by a regular jury. . . . Excepting on festive days, they dress after the manner of the white man, but far more picturesquely. They live in small log houses of their own construction, and have everything they need or desire in the way of food.[22]

Today the Eastern Band of Cherokee Indians has grown to about nine thousand people and holds 56,572 acres of communal lands in Swain, Jackson, Cherokee, and Graham Counties.[23] The decades following removal were not without difficulty, however, for the traditionalist Cherokees who had been left behind. A crop failure in 1836 and the confiscation of Cherokee goods in 1838 by the removal army had created a situation of starvation during the removal period.[24] The federal government did not recognize the Cherokees' right to remain in the east until 1842, and it was 1866 before the state recognized their right, or that of any non-whites, to own land. Periods of disfranchisement were common during this era. From 1840 to 1848 the Eastern Cherokees gave refuge to the South Carolina Catawba Indians who were also in danger of removal. The Civil War years of the early 1860s saw the North Carolina Cherokees, who sent off most of their young men to war, split into pro-Confederacy and pro-Union factions that disrupted the tribe. The loss of lives during the war years was followed by yet another smallpox epidemic in 1866 with a further loss of lives (over a hundred people).

The major problem which affected all Eastern Cherokees from removal through the 1880s, and even beyond, was land. In 1866, the same year the state recognized the Cherokees' right to own land, the Cherokees almost lost most of their North Carolina holdings. William Thomas, the trusted white man who had held their lands in his name, became seriously ill, and as his health failed, so did his business interests. Those to whom he owed money sued, and they made no distinction between Thomas' own property and that he held in trust for the Cherokees. Court cases followed in abundance.

By the 1860s the Graham County Snowbird Cherokee area included four hundred fullblood Cherokees, and in 1868 the North Carolina Cherokees, with a total population of more than seventeen hundred, met at Cheoah, or Snowbird, in general council and took the preliminary steps toward establishing a constitution and reasserting their legal status over their lands.[25] This constitution was inaugurated in 1870 when the first principal chief, Flying Squirrel (Saunooke), was elected. The fact that the first general council of the Eastern Cherokees since removal was held at Cheoah demonstrates the importance of the Snowbird Cherokee area. In addition, the second man elected principal chief was Lloyd R. Welch, in 1875, who was from Snowbird.[26]

Finally, in 1886 the United States Supreme Court ruled that the North Carolina and Oklahoma Cherokees legally and politically were two separate groups. Efforts to encourage the Cherokees in the east to remove west officially ceased, and in 1889 the Eastern Band of Cherokee Indians was recognized as a corporation under North Carolina laws, with the federal government acting as trustee for their lands, which gained federal reservation status.

The Snowbird community of Cheoah was a significant group among the post-removal North Carolina Cherokees. Besides being the site of the council which took the first steps toward organizing the Eastern Band of Cherokee Indians, Cheoah was important enough to have a trading post nearby at Fort Montgomery, now Robbinsville. The store was one of seven operated by William Thomas that were begun during the removal years and continued until the Civil War. In 1880, when the Graham County Cherokee population numbered 189, the Society of Friends located one of their newly established day schools for Cherokee children at Cheoah.

Although in the post-removal years the Snowbird Indians in Graham County were just as much Cherokee traditionalists as those on the Qualla Boundary, who numbered more than eight hundred in 1880, there were significant differences between the two groups. From aboriginal times the two groups had spoken separate dialects of Cherokee: Atali in Cheoah and Kituhwa in the Boundary area.[27] After 1819 the Cherokees of the Qualla Boundary area were no longer on the land of the Cherokee Nation and not subject to the 1838 removal of the Cherokee Nation. Cheoah was within the Nation, in the Aquohee District, and clearly in danger of removal. Among Euchella's band of fugitives was a man named "Wa-chu-cha" (or Wachacha), a Cherokee name common today only in Snowbird. To avoid immediate removal it was necessary for many of those in Cheoah to purchase from North Carolina lands on which they were already living.

Following the removal, one large tract of land, the Qualla Boundary, today comprising 45,413 acres, and a nearby smaller area, the Thomas Tract, the so-called Thirty-two Hundred Acre Tract, were established for those Cherokees in the Swain and Jackson County areas.[28] The same was never established for the Snowbird Cherokees in the Graham County area fifty miles to the southwest: "At one time it was intended by Thomas and the Indians in the area of Cheoih [Cheoah] to purchase a general boundary of land in that section [Graham County] to be known as the Cheoih Boundary. They signed an agreement to this effect, but as the Indians declined to furnish the funds needed to make the purchase, the boundary was never acquired. Some of the Indians purchased individual tracts from Thomas and other owners."[29] Those individual tracts today number 2,249 acres. A similar system of individual tracts developed in Cherokee County to the south where today 5,571 acres are in Cherokee hands.[30] Systems of individual tracts, a dramatically different situation than that on the Boundary, meant a less than isolated situation for Snowbird Indians, as Indian Agent John A. Sibbald commented in 1880: "There are but few white men living inside of the Qualla Boundary, but in Graham, Cherokee, and Macon Counties the Indians live among the whites, and are fairly treated."[31]

The relative isolation of the Qualla Boundary, however, did not last long after Sibbald made that statement. A white population influx (an echo of a similar white immigration a hundred years earlier) as well as the permanent establishment of schools, both beginning in the late nineteenth century, ended the Boundary's racial and cultural isolation. Lured by the hope of obtaining ownership of "free" Indian land through allotment under the federally initiated Dawes Act, many whites claimed minimal Cherokee ancestry and moved onto parts of the reservation in the 1880s and 1890s.[32] These individuals and the whites who began intermarrying with Qualla Cherokees in the 1880s are the ancestors of today's white Indians. By contrast, the first Indian-white intermarriage in Snowbird did not occur until around 1960, and even in the 1990s white Indians are still virtually non-existent in Snowbird.

Local whites poorly understood Indian issues, and the *Asheville Times*, the regional newspaper for western North Carolina, asked in May 1923: "Are the Cherokees united in their opinion that the land should be allotted to them directly [as private property]?" Eastern Cherokees living out of state and anyone who believed they might have any Indian blood,

Cherokee or otherwise, wrote to the superintendent to ask for a share of money or land. Eastern Cherokees justifiably felt insecure about their futures, with allotment hanging over them. For decades Cherokees feared that under allotment communally owned lands might be divided up into private tracts and that the property on which one family had a house and possessions might be assigned to another family. In 1931 the local Indian superintendent wrote about a Cherokee man in the Snow-bird community who was "wondering now if it is safe to go ahead and improve the holding with the view of having his allotment made out of this tract and covering the land which he will improve, provided, of course, allotments are ever made."[33] Needless to say, the era was not made any less dismal by the Great Depression of the 1930s or even World War I when some Cherokees were drafted in spite of the fact that they were not then United States citizens and supposedly not subject to the draft.

Intensifying before the turn of the century and continuing into the 1920s, logging had offered some hope of economic independence.[34] With a growing population in economic need, however, Cherokee timber was soon being overcut. For all practical purposes the lumber industry was dead by the depression. The enforcement of stock fencing laws also drastically reduced the number of animals being raised, and the number of family farms decreased as well.

Land disputes, due to overpopulation and threat of allotment, increased on the Cherokee reservation. More and more individuals of minimal Cherokee blood, or none at all, were challenged when they attempted to enroll as Eastern Cherokees.

Although the 1880 United States census counted 1,105 Cherokees in the four major counties having Indian population, the 1884 Hester Roll enumerated 1,881 Eastern Cherokees in North Carolina, or a jump of 776 people in only four years.[35] In reference to the Hester Roll, which enumerated an additional 1,075 Cherokees in more than a half dozen other eastern states besides North Carolina, anthropologist James Mooney wrote: "Although the census received the approval and certificate of the Eastern Cherokee council, a large portion of the band still refuse to recognize it as authoritative, claiming that a large number of persons therein enrolled have no Cherokee blood."[36] Even as late as 1929 the Eastern Cherokee writer Henry Owl could remark: "The enrollment [culminating in the Baker Roll of 1931] took a sudden spurt in 1929 because of the plans for allotment, and many names on the list will not stand too close scrutiny for eligibility."[37] In fact, Tribal Council contested over 1,200 of the 3,146 people finally enrolled.[38] White-Indian intermarriage also seems to have increased during this period, drastically changing the once almost totally fullblood North Carolina Cherokee population into one with a large number of white Indians. Parts of the Qualla Boundary, as well as most of the Cherokee County area, seem to have been affected by the white onslaught much more than the more rugged Snowbird area in Graham County ever was. Being the largest population, the more accessible areas of the Qualla Boundary (Yellow Hill, Birdtown, and Painttown) were the logical focus for this onslaught. Today most of the main reservation's fertile bottomlands, which are located along the major tourist routes, are controlled by white Indians.

The Cherokee County area in many respects had always been tied more to the progressive spirit of the Georgia Cherokee hill country than to the conservative spirit of the North Carolina Cherokee mountains; missions and schools had a pre-removal date in Cherokee County, as in Georgia. So it is suspected that the white onslaught there may have occurred even earlier than on the Boundary, probably one hundred years earlier, in the late eighteenth or early nineteenth centuries. The Swetland Roll of 1869 lists most of the five hundred Indians in the Cherokee County area as minimal-blood-degree Cherokees, while the twelve hundred Indians on the Qualla Boundary and in Snowbird were listed as fullbloods.[39]

Largely as a result of the white population influx in the 1880s and 1890s, there was less good land to go around to all enrolled Eastern Cherokees. Two travelers, William Zeigler and Ben Grosscup, in 1883 noted that "the fields, originally of average fertility, are worn out by bad farming probably due to the population pressure on too little land."[40] This contrasts with traveler Charles Lanman's description of pre-white influx Cherokees who "have everything they need or desire in the way of food."[41]

Formal education, begun in 1880 by the Society of Friends, or Quakers, began modifying North Carolina Cherokee culture, just as other mission schools had done in the north Georgia area almost a century before. Although the completion of the conversion to Christianity of North Carolina Cherokees had taken place largely before 1880, the process had not changed many fundamental aspects of Cherokee culture. This was probably the result of the Baptist Church, dominant among the post-removal Cherokees, which quickly put Indians in positions of authority on the local level, thus minimizing white-Indian contact through the churches.[42]

With the Quakers' establishment of five day schools for elementary students and a coeducational boarding school for secondary students, the acculturation process accelerated.

Before 1880 the tendency had been to assimilate the small numbers of white Indian children into Cherokee culture. After 1880 not only had the actual numbers of whites and white Indians increased, but the schools were emphasizing Anglo-American values rather than Cherokee culture, and the tendency to assimilate whites and white Indians into Cherokee culture shifted to a tendency to assimilate Cherokees into Anglo-American culture. The presence of white parents in the homes and white teachers in the schools worked together to emphasize Anglo-American culture over Cherokee culture.

In 1892 Quaker control of Cherokee schools was relinquished to the federal government under which acculturation was rapidly accelerated, largely through the extensive use of out-of-state boarding schools. It is interesting that the Swetland Roll of 1869 makes references to the Qualla Boundary where "they [the Cherokees] . . . maintain a school with two teachers who teach both languages" and to Snowbird where "they maintain a school most of the time."[43] This reference to pre-Quaker, bilingual schools operated by the Cherokees themselves indicates that formal education among the Eastern Cherokees has not always been in the hands of outsiders and that the schools became a powerful force for acculturation only after their control fell into the hands of non-Indians. Unfortunately, no known descriptions of these schools and their instructional programs exist, and the schools themselves ceased to exist during the period immediately before the establishment of schools by the Society of Friends.

During the first two decades of the twentieth century the role of the Bureau of Indian Affairs in Cherokee schools bordered on the dictatorial. White teachers became the norm and boarding schools the ideal. Children were beaten for speaking the Cherokee language and encouraged to adopt white cultural patterns to the exclusion of those Cherokee. A heavy emphasis was placed on vocational education although Cherokees often had more difficulty in finding decent jobs than whites with less education. Runaways were a constant problem among Cherokee students. With the possible exception of the "New Deal" era, the goal of federal education was to change Cherokee culture dramatically. Even an attempt under Commissioner of Indian Affairs John Collier's "Indian New Deal" to teach the dying Cherokee language in the schools failed, ironically because some Cherokees themselves, mostly white Indians educated at boarding schools, viewed the language experiment as a return to "savagery." By the 1950s formal education was officially back on an acculturationist track.

For American Indians generally the beginning of the twentieth century meant their population was finally beginning to increase again, after four hundred years of steady decline. There were still problems, however, and diseases still plagued Indian areas. The Cherokees were often hit hard by severe bouts of influenza. Shortly before 1920 the swine flu epidemic engulfed the Cherokee area, taking many lives. About the same time, a whooping cough epidemic struck Chilocco Boarding School in Oklahoma and an unnamed disease killed many Indian students at Haskell Boarding School in Kansas. Many Cherokees attended both schools. Letters to and from the superintendent at Cherokee mention tuberculosis as well.

As late as 1930, Cherokee Indians were not being allowed to vote by the state of North Carolina, although in the Cherokee area itself, one county permitted resident Cherokees to vote, while neighboring counties refused.[44] Cherokees were having problems with land taxes as well. In 1925 one U.S. District Court judge ruled that the federal act of 1924, making Indians United States citizens, exempted reservation land from taxation. The next year, however, the local counties again tried to tax reservation land. In the ensuing court case, a different judge ruled that Indian land could be taxed. By 1931 the Cherokee case was on its way to the U.S. Supreme Court, still unsettled. Some Indian families, unable to pay their taxes, lost their land. More land would have been lost, but the Tribal Council sometimes was able to pay the back taxes: "It seems that the Eastern Band of Cherokee Indians through its council seeks to pay the taxes of lands in Graham County [Snowbird] owned by the individual members of the Band. These Indians have fallen behind in their tax payments and are unable to pay same . . . it now becomes necessary to act or the Indians will in all probability lose their lands. . . . The tribe has a sufficient amount ($300) to take care of the taxes involved and there is no question of its desire to do so."[45]

With the closing of the Cherokee boarding school in 1954, all Qualla Boundary students were bused daily to and from Cherokee High School. For Snowbird Cherokees, the school's demise had a different effect. Up until 1954 Snowbird students going on to high school had no other choice than boarding schools, either fifty miles away on the main reservation or out of state. Many Snowbird people thus never graduated from high school. With the closing of the Qualla Boundary boarding school, Snowbird Cherokees had no official high school, and the new day high school on Qualla was too far away for daily busing (over a hundred miles, round-trip). So all Snowbird Cherokee students began attending Graham County's major public school, Robbinsville High, with white students. The integration of Indian students into the previously all-white school was accomplished with the aid of the Bureau of Indian Affairs which still pays the school system an annual set fee per student. Special programs, such as the one on the Cherokee language, are sometimes provided to Indian students at Robbinsville High out of federal funds.

Until 1965 Snowbird children still attended an all-Indian BIA day school for the elementary grades where, at least to each other, they could speak the Cherokee language in the small two-teacher establishment. In 1965 Snowbird became the last of the community day schools on the reservation to close, and elementary school children from Snowbird began attending the county public schools along with the older high school students who had been doing so for the previous eleven years.

During the twentieth century several other factors besides education have encouraged culture change. Prominent among these factors have been depressing economic trends. In the mid-nineteenth century, before population increases placed excessive demands on the limited land base, most Cherokees adequately provided for their needs by farming. Yet by 1908 most Cherokees were reported as living in poverty because, as a government official stated: "there are few opportunities in that part of North Carolina where they live for them to earn money, and they are obliged to depend upon their sterile little farms."[46]

As the population has steadily increased, with no corresponding increases in the size of the reservation, the Eastern Cherokees have been able to depend less and less on farming as a means of livelihood. By the

1950s only about 10 percent of the people supported themselves by farming, and by the 1970s not one Cherokee family received its livelihood from that source.[47]

This decline in farming has meant that more Cherokees have turned to other occupations, which often has taken them off the reservation into wage labor. World War II, Korea, and Vietnam have taken numerous Cherokee men away from North Carolina and exposed them to the larger world. Many of these veterans have later moved away from the reservation in their search for jobs, or commuted daily to jobs in neighboring areas by automobile.

If the automobile has had a significant acculturative role by providing transportation for Cherokees going off the reservation, it has also had a tremendous effect on the economy of the reservation itself. During the post-World War II prosperity decades, more and more Americans began vacationing by car. Due to their location near the Great Smoky Mountains National Park, the country's most visited national park, the Cherokees experienced an annual summer influx of millions of tourists eager to see "real Indians."

By the 1950s tourism provided more income to the reservation than any other single source of employment, but it still was not adequate. Tourism provided many jobs, so that unemployment during the summer dropped to only 1 percent. But most of these jobs were low-paying and limited to the summer months. During the winter, unemployment soared to 20 percent more than the national average.[48] In 1958 the local BIA Superintendent, Richard Butts, wrote that because of the "dire need" among the Cherokees, there was "much actual hunger."[49]

By the 1970s some economic progress had been made, and Cherokee incomes had increased to 60 percent of the national average, but most families needed to have more than one family member employed just to make ends meet.[50] The potential impact of the tourist trade has been diluted because one-third of the tourist enterprises, comprising the largest money-making shops (complete with fake Indian crafts made in Haiti or other poor Third World countries), are owned by non-Indians. The reservation's dependence on tourism has also made it hard hit by gasoline shortages, high gasoline prices, national unemployment rates, inflation, and the recessionary trends of the 1970s and 1980s, all of which have affected the ability of Americans to take vacations.

Tourism, however, has centered on the Qualla Boundary so that most

Snowbird Cherokees who do participate in the enterprise must move to the Boundary during the summer or commute about a hundred miles round-trip each day. Some Snowbird women make high-quality native baskets, a traditional Cherokee activity, for sale at the tribal cooperative, Qualla Arts and Crafts, and this activity does not require them to come in contact with tourists themselves.[51] Few Snowbird Cherokee individuals are directly affected by tourism, and many are engaged in various types of non-tourism wage labor. Since 1982 Snowbird and other Cherokee communities have benefited from the money flowing into tribal government from high-stakes bingo operated on the Qualla Boundary. As with craft production, bingo is an aspect of the tourism economy which economically benefits Snowbird people while keeping them physically isolated from tourists.

Despite continuing economic problems and pressures for culture change, Cherokees have retained a strong hold on their ethnic identity. This identity is primarily the result of a continuing strong cultural tradition, especially among fullbloods, that refuses to disappear. No matter what the blood degree or cultural outlook of an individual Cherokee is, however, there are advantages to identifying ethnically as a Cherokee Indian. Many of the advantages are economic. The most basic economic advantage for members of the Eastern Band of Cherokee Indians is access to reservation land. Still legally a corporation under North Carolina laws, the Band's assets consist of its lands, with the Band's members functioning as stockholders. Although reservation lands cannot be "owned," individual Band members can have "possessory rights" to tracts of land which can be sold to, bought from, willed to, or inherited from any other Band member. Inherited reservation land compares favorably with expensive off-reservation land and high rents in nearby towns. Many Cherokees can survive more inexpensively by living in homes on the reservation and commuting long distances to find work than by moving closer to their off-reservation jobs.

In recent years another major economic advantage has been provided to those possessing reservation tracts. In 1962 the Qualla Housing Authority was formed, and in its first decade of operation the authority arranged for over four hundred houses to be built or significantly improved, reducing the fraction of substandard housing from nearly 90 to less than 60 percent.[52] By 1990 the total number of new houses exceeded eleven hundred. To qualify for a new house under this program at least one member of a household must have possessory rights to a tract of land upon which the house can be built.

Many Indians and whites in the southern Appalachians are not well off economically, and low-cost, good quality housing encourages many who can qualify to establish their Band membership. There have been other economic lures to identifying ethnically as a Cherokee Indian in the latter half of the twentieth century. One notable lure is the Band's successful suit, settled in 1972, for a government land claims payment of nearly two million dollars for all Cherokee lands permanently lost to whites. Another economic incentive is the financial success of high-stakes bingo, begun a decade later in 1982. These kinds of economic advantages encouraged the white Indian community of Tomotla in Cherokee County to invade politically the real Indian Snowbird community in 1973.

Today there is a slowly growing awareness of Indian identity among the Eastern Cherokees. For many it is an effort to maintain a simultaneous identity as "real Americans" and "real Indians." Each summer in the Snowbird community, isolated from the tourist onslaught, the Trail of Tears Singing takes place, and the Cherokee language lives again. Each autumn, after the tourist season, the Eastern Cherokees hold their Fall Festival. Other Indians from as far away as New Mexico, Florida, Oklahoma, and New York attend, further reducing the Eastern Cherokees' isolation, not only from the world of white Americans but from other Native Americans as well. After the 1972 Fall Festival, at the height of the nationwide Red Power Movement, the *Cherokee One Feather* ran an article which proclaimed: "The old fair has become a festival, and 'festival' means 'sharing, celebration, and ceremony.' . . . The major attractions at the Fall Festival were ethnic: Indian customs, culture and self image. Perhaps one bumper sticker summed it up: 'Brothers, rejoice! It's *in* to be Indian!' "[53] Traditional stickball games and booger dances, thought to have been acculturated out of existence, are performed—alongside ferris wheels and cotton candy concessions, but they are performed.

Cultural traditionalism may be on the upswing, perhaps as a result of the 1970s Red Power Movement, but the Eastern Cherokee economy is not doing as well despite housing opportunities, government money, and bingo. Perhaps because of such economic conditions, in 1972 the Eastern Band of Cherokee Indians voted to accept the offer from the

Indian Claims Commission of nearly two million dollars for all Cherokee lands permanently lost to whites. For two decades the Eastern Band
struggled with this government commission over a settlement. A general council, the first since the one at Snowbird in 1868, was held on the
Qualla Boundary to take the vote. At the meeting the council accepted
the government's offer of money, but one young man urged that land,
not money, be returned to the Cherokees. His comment received a round
of applause. This is not surprising, since the major issue confronting the
Eastern Cherokees today, as during the removal period, is land: how to
hold onto it, how to use it, how to increase it, and who should have access
to it.

CURRENT SITUATION

In the Snowbird community many institutions today are in Indian control: four churches, Buffalo, Zion Hill, and Little Snowbird, all Baptist,
and the Church of the Lamb, interdenominational; the Snowbird Rescue
Squad; Snowbird Health Clinic; Snowbird Volunteer Fire Department;
Snowbird Funeral Association; Trail of Tears Singing Organization;
Snowbird Library; Snowbird Community Store; Ed Jackson Scholarship
Fund; and Snowbird Community Development Club, to name but the
most obvious. The Snowbird Community Club apparently absorbed an
older community service organization, the *gadugi*, or free labor company,
whose origins go back to aboriginal times.[54] Among the Eastern Band,
the *gadugi* was a group of people from a community who organized communal labor, mostly relating to the cooperative planting and harvesting
of every family's crops and assisting people during times of illness or
death. In the twentieth century many of these *gadugis* developed formal
structures with officers elected or, in Snowbird's case, chosen by the
more traditional method of consensus. The *gadugi* leader was termed
a "captain." With the coming of community development clubs which
could tap into some government funds in the post–World War II era,
some communities, like Big Cove, experienced more factionalism as a
result. White Indians joined the community development clubs, while
fullbloods remained in the *gadugis*. This was not the case for Snowbird
where the *gadugi* and its functions were absorbed into the local community club and overlapping funeral association. The Snowbird Community

Club is quite successful, and in 1971, for example, it was awarded first prize in a Western North Carolina Community Development Program contest.

Snowbird also participates in institutional frameworks not of the community's making. The most important of these institutions are the Graham County Public Schools, which Indian children now attend. Most Snowbird people are also employed by companies or economic programs operated by whites.

Probably the most pressing problem facing the Eastern Cherokees today is the inadequate land base of the reservation. It affects every community, including Snowbird. Although the amount of land controlled by the Eastern Band has not varied significantly since the removal of 1838, the number of people using the land has increased more than ninefold, from about one thousand to more than nine thousand. In addition, the land itself has become more sterile over the years. With too little land to go around, even close kinsmen openly bicker with each other and argue land inheritance cases before Tribal Council. Such controversies involve fullbloods as well as white Indians. When usually non-aggressive traditionalist Cherokees act aggressively, land controversies are often involved. In these cases, the traditional value system based on harmony seems to take a back seat to the pressing economic concerns generated by the shortage of land.

Despite land controversies, Snowbird Cherokees generally ascribe to the very real traditional value system which anthropologists have termed the Harmony Ethic. The Harmony Ethic is in fact a major characteristic by means of which the Snowbird community asserts its "real Indian" identity. The Harmony Ethic's basic features include first, non-aggressiveness and non-competitiveness, particularly if the goal of aggressiveness is individual success. The use of intermediaries, or neutral third parties, is important in minimizing face-to-face hostility in interpersonal relations. Generosity is another important characteristic, and it occurs even when people cannot afford to be generous. A concept of immanent justice relieves people from feelings of needing to control others through direct interference.[55]

There is, therefore, much that is traditional about the Snowbird community. Many traditional traits are quite noticeable, like speaking the Cherokee language or the manufacture of Indian crafts. Others, like the practicing of herbal medicine by Indian doctors (conjurers) or the belief in a value system based on harmony, are either intentionally hidden or not as noticeable to outsiders taking only a superficial glimpse at the community. Snowbird's unique history has served to perpetuate a variety of these traditional traits.

GEOGRAPHY

Originally an isolated part of Cherokee County to the south, Graham County, the home of the Snowbird Cherokees, was formed in 1872. The county is one of the most mountainous in North Carolina, and only one other county has less of its land cleared for farming and industry. The mountains, some over five thousand feet high, that ring the county do not enclose broad bottomlands but rather sharp ridges and deep, swift creeks. The ruggedness of the landscape is enhanced by large expanses of forest, some of it virgin, which cover more than 85 percent of the county. Some of the indigenous hardwoods that have been the basis of the county's small lumbering businesses are oaks, hemlocks, and poplars. Pines grow on cut-over lands, and there is an undergrowth of mountain laurel, rhododendron, dogwoods, and sourwoods. Adding to Graham County's image as a rugged area are the native animals, which included bears, deer, bobcats, and "panthers" (eastern mountain lions) as well as a thriving import, wild boars.

Still a sparsely populated area (in the 1980 census only 7,217 people), the Graham County region was settled only after other areas in the state had been claimed. Whites moved into the area, often called "North Carolina's last frontier," late and in small numbers. For decades both white and Cherokee farmers engaged in subsistence agriculture and did not attempt to transport cash crops out of the mountains to market.

Although today some wheat, hay, corn, potatoes, and tobacco are grown, and some cattle, hogs, and poultry are raised, most crops and livestock are for home consumption, and farming as a paying occupation is relatively unimportant. Only about 6 percent of Graham County land is suitable for cultivation. So Graham County residents, both whites and Cherokees, seek employment in wage labor.

Local employment is largely the result of obvious environmental conditions and opportunities: some lumbering, in the past some dam building, land-clearing, power company employment, saw-mill enterprises, a furniture plant, and some tourism (as a result of the area's natural beauty rather than because of the resident Indians). A few smaller companies, some service enterprises, the schools, and some professional employment comprise the other sources of labor in the region.

The Graham County climate is temperate, but because of the altitude, nights are quite cool, even in the summer. The rate of rainfall is high, especially in the summer, and the high humidity lends a perpetual atmosphere of dampness to the area. Unless it is an unusually mild winter, several snowfalls occur from late fall to early spring.

The present white population is largely comprised of the descendants of nineteenth- and early twentieth-century immigrants to the region from other areas of the southeast. The region is not thriving economically, and few outsiders, other than a few retirees and those building summer vacation cottages, move in as permanent, year-round residents. The southern mountains never supported a viable slave-operated, plantation economy, and there is thus no permanent black population in Graham County. Like whites, outside blacks are not especially attracted to the area for any economic reasons, and Graham is the only North Carolina county with no permanent black residents whatsoever. Graham County's population growth has not changed significantly in the past third of a century as United States Census Bureau figures show: in 1950, 6,886 people; in 1960, 6,432; in 1970, 6,562; and in 1980, 7,217. Despite a relatively high reproductive rate, emigration from the county prevents significant population growth.

SNOWBIRD'S ADAPTATION

Snowbird Cherokees are only 5.2 percent of Graham County's population. They are 6.9 percent of all resident North Carolina Cherokees. So, whether in relation to local whites or other Eastern Cherokees, the Snowbird community is a small minority. What will be demonstrated in the following chapters is how the Snowbird community is able to maintain a clear-cut, positive identity as a "real" Cherokee Indian community, despite its minority status, relative isolation from other Cherokees and other Indians in general, and an intense interaction with white Americans since removal days.

Snowbird, more than anything else, is a successful community. It is successful, and it is adaptive. Snowbird continues in the tradition of a generalized adaptation that has meant survival for the Cherokees over the centuries. Like their historic and prehistoric ancestors, Snowbird Cherokees tap many resources in both their natural and social environment without becoming exclusively dependent on any. They garden, gather, fish, and hunt. Sometimes they raise chickens or pigs. Most look to wage labor as well, and some dabble in tourist-related enterprises. Politically they are adept at tapping the resources of Band, county, state, and nation, as well as private sources of funding. Because they are not dependent on any one factor or group, they survive with as many of their Cherokee traits as they choose to preserve. And they choose to preserve a great deal.

2

"Real Indians"

Overleaf: Traditional crafts such as the beadworking of fullblood Martha Wachacha thrive in Snowbird. Basketmaking, native medicine, and the Cherokee language are other surviving traditions.

Photo courtesy of the Museum of the Cherokee Indian.

IN SPITE OF SIGNIFICANT CULTURE CHANGE, the Snowbird Cherokees offer an ideal situation for the study of ethnic persistence, successful
group adaptation, and ethnic relations. Nearly all observers of Cherokee culture, whether missionaries, educators, governmental bureaucrats,
travelers, or, more recently, anthropologists and other social scientists,
have shared one main premise about Cherokee society: their conviction
that it has been modified almost to the point of oblivion. (The Cherokees were thus long ago termed the "most civilized" of the Five Civilized
Tribes of the Southeast.)

Holding this attitude, anthropologists like James Mooney and
William H. Gilbert worked to save or reconstruct what they could
of aboriginal Cherokee culture. Others, like Leonard Bloom, gave up
trying to find "real" Cherokee culture and criticized the Bureau of Indian
Affairs for delaying the Cherokees' assimilated destiny. Recent studies
include John Gulick's and Harriet J. Kupferer's worthwhile efforts to
discover the remaining subtleties that distinguish Cherokee culture from
the white American culture of the southern Appalachians.[1]

Although many white American observers of the Cherokees have for
more than a century and a half predicted the society's demise as a result of cultural changes, the Cherokees have persisted as an identifiable
group. This is despite the efforts of assimilationist factions, the diminish-
ment of the Cherokees' geographic isolation, their forced participation
in white American culture via schools and other institutions, the loss
of individual members to non-Indian society, and the addition of non-
Indian members to Cherokee society.[2]

An analysis of culture change does not adequately explain the Cherokees' persistence. Therefore, a new premise and a new approach to the
study of Cherokee society is now warranted. Anthropologist Fredrik
Barth in particular has urged more fieldwork on ethnic group persistence: "What is required is a combined theoretical and empirical attack:
we need to investigate closely the empirical facts of a variety of cases."[3]
The Snowbird Cherokees are an excellent example of such a case. It is
hoped an examination of this group will shed light on ethnic persistence
in general. In later chapters situational analysis is used as the major
method in this examination.

There are also pragmatic justifications for examining a group like
Snowbird. A study of ethnic persistence and interethnic relations fills
a practical need for Cherokees and Native Americans generally. While

other ethnic groups within the United States, especially African Americans, have been inundated with studies of their "race" relations, studies of Native American ethnic relations are comparatively few. Sioux Indian author and attorney Vine Deloria, Jr., for example, has frequently expressed the fear that generalizations about white-black relations will be seized upon as the model for all white-minority group relations and that the problems peculiar to white-red relations will thus be misinterpreted. Writing in the days before Wounded Knee Two, after which the Indian situation has become better known, Deloria suggested: "Indian people have not become well known in the field of inter-group and race relations. Consequently they have suffered from the attitudes of people who have only a superficial knowledge of minority groups and have attached a certain stigma to them."[4] In addition, echoing James Mooney's call in the 1880s, anthropologist John Gulick has specifically urged a study of the Snowbird community: "The lack of systematically gathered material from Snowbird is regrettable, for the people of Snowbird are reported to include a larger number of . . . Conservatives . . . far less affected by the tourist business."[5]

INTERETHNIC RELATIONS

Although a small black population is present in the southern North Carolina mountains, the two main ethnic groups are white Appalachians and Cherokee Indians. Nowhere in the southern Appalachians do these two ethnic groups have more intense relations while successfully maintaining their separate identities than in the Snowbird Mountain Range of Graham County, North Carolina. In Graham County, especially in the area around Snowbird Creek, Little Snowbird Creek, and Buffalo Creek, Cherokee-owned and white-owned land lots are interspersed in almost checkerboard fashion. Largely because the Cherokee land lots (2,249 acres in twenty-three original tracts which form thirteen distinct blocks of land) constitute federally supervised Indian reservation lands and therefore cannot be sold to non-Cherokees, the ethnic checkerboard has been preserved through time. This system of land tenure has guaranteed intense interethnic relations by insuring that individuals from each ethnic group have neighbors from the other group while also protecting the minority Cherokees from encroachments by whites. The situation is different fifty miles to the northeast where Qualla Boundary Cherokees

Changing North Carolina Cherokee Indian Population Figures by County

Year	Graham County (Snowbird)	Cherokee County (Tomotla)	Jackson County (Painttown & Wolfetown)	Swain County (Big Cove, Yellow Hill & Birdtown)	Total
1880	189 (17.1%)	98 (8.9%)	377 (34.1%)	441 (39.9%)	1,105
1890	no data	no data	no data	no data	no data
1900	127 (9.2%)	37 (2.7%)	340 (24.6%)	875 (63.4%)	1,379
1910	157 (10.8%)	31 (2.1%)	450 (31.0%)	812 (56.0%)	1,450
1920	156 (9.7%)	14 (0.9%)	576 (35.8%)	864 (53.7%)	1,610
1930	42 (2.4%)	60 (3.5%)	553 (32.2%)	1,060 (61.8%)	1,715
1940	172 (7.1%)	29 (1.2%)	841 (34.9%)	1,368 (56.8%)	2,410
1950	209 (7.7%)	24 (0.9%)	1,054 (39.1%)	1,411 (52.3%)	2,698
1960	255 (7.7%)	62 (1.9%)	1,397 (42.2%)	1,596 (48.2%)	3,310
1970	320 (9.9%)	71 (2.1%)	1,858 (57.2%)	996 (30.1%)	3,245*
1980	379 (6.9%)	189 (3.4%)	2,412 (44.0%)	2,502 (45.6%)	5,482*

Source: Adapted from data provided to the author by the Bureau of the Census, U.S. Department of Commerce. Population data before 1880 is not included because the Graham County area was part of Cherokee County, and thus population sub-totals were not distinguished.

*The official 1970 U.S. Census figure for the four North Carolina counties which contain Cherokee Indian residents is far below the 1972 estimate of Cherokee Indian population made by tribal government in *Cherokee Progress and Challenge*, which reported "over 7,000 enrolled members, with an estimated 5,000 living on or immediately adjacent to the Cherokee Indian lands." The most probable reason for this significant discrepancy is that many white Indians were self-identifying as whites on the 1970 U.S. Census, and as Indians on the Band enrollment during an era when several economic benefits became available to those who could establish tribal membership. By 1980 more people were self-identifying as Indians, and the largest jump in Eastern Cherokee population ever recorded by the U.S. Census occurred between 1970 and 1980 when the North Carolina Cherokee population grew by 68.9 percent. The largest percentage jump was in the white Indian community in Cherokee County whose population grew by 166.2 percent. Self-identification by ethnic group began with the 1960 U.S. Census.

own two large blocks of land (one of 45,414 acres and one of 3,200 acres) surrounded by whites. Thirty miles to the southwest, Cherokee Indians in Cherokee County also own scattered tracts of land (5,571 acres), but other factors have created different social situations for Graham and Cherokee County Indians.

As part of Graham County, the Snowbird Cherokee community participates in the local political system by voting in elections, serving on juries and committees, presenting disputes to the courts for judgment, and participating in political parties, to name but a few of the more obvious means of participation. The community also interacts with neighboring white communities in local wage labor and in the public school system. Cherokees and whites must interact in the classroom from at least age six to sixteen and later in life at their jobs when they become co-workers.

INTRAETHNIC RELATIONS

Snowbird Cherokees do not, however, orient themselves only toward Graham County and their white neighbors. The Snowbird community is also part of the Cheoah Township, one of six such political units on the Eastern Cherokee reservation, the other five being located on the Qualla Boundary. Each township elects two representatives to Tribal Council every other year. Elections are held in September during odd-numbered years.

The Snowbird community participates in the tribal political system by, for example, voting in elections; serving on committees; participating in special-interest political groups; and presenting land claims cases, wills, and other tribal matters before council for judgment. The community also shares with other Cherokee communities opportunities for tribal employment, a medical system operated by the Indian Health Service, a house-building program, land claims money, and bingo profits. It is the Snowbird community's political affiliation with the Eastern Band of Cherokee Indians, as a unit of land, the Cheoah Township, as well as a unit of people, that prohibits the sale of Cherokee lands in Graham County to non-Indians and creates the unique land tenure system in the county. Thus, the Snowbird community must relate to both Graham County and the Eastern Band in land tenure, political, economic, and educational systems, to cite only the most obvious aspects of inter-community relations.

Graham County and the Eastern Band of Cherokee Indians each have populations numbering around eight thousand. Thus the Snowbird community, numbering about 380 as of the 1980 census, interacts with two groups of people each numerically larger. Despite this, the community maintains a clear image of itself as the Snowbird Cherokee community and not merely as a segment of two larger systems. Snowbird successfully interacts with various ethnic groups while maintaining its cultural traditionalism, such as its high percentage of fullbloods, Cherokee-language speakers, native craftsmen, and Indian doctors.

INTERTRIBAL RELATIONS

Not only does the community actively interact with local white Appalachians and other Cherokees but it has taken the lead in interacting with another Indian tribe, the Western Cherokees from Oklahoma, and in the process Snowbird is helping to diminish the entire Eastern Band's isolation from other Native Americans. Although there are no political or economic bonds with the Western Cherokees, as with Graham County and the Eastern Band, there are cultural ties, especially religious, linguistic, artistic, and historical ones, by which Snowbird and other Eastern Cherokee communities are seeking to renew relations with Cherokees in Oklahoma.

Snowbird Cherokees also directly participate, as citizens, in the state of North Carolina and the United States, mostly by voting in elections. Most of the community's relations with North Carolina are indirect, however, via Graham County. The community's relations with the federal government are also largely indirect, via tribal government.

ETHNIC PERSISTENCE

In the case of the Snowbird community, adaptation to the larger non-Indian or non-traditionalist world has not led to assimilation but has resulted in a condition of ethnic persistence and only limited, strategically adaptive culture change. Culture change without total assimilation is not an entirely new concept. Harald Eidheim has described the persistence of Lapp ethnic identity in the face of acculturation by Norway, and surrounding the Lappish Movement are circumstances reminiscent of the Red Power Movement in North America. Anthony F. C. Wallace's study of revitalization movements, particularly among the Seneca Indians and other Iroquois groups, implicitly assumes that ethnic identities do not necessarily have to become assimilated out of existence. John J. Honigmann, in describing Cree Indian and Eskimo relations in Canada, suggests that satisfactory symbiotic relations can develop between ethnic groups and bolster each group's persistence rather than causing their assimilation. Thus, various alternatives to assimilation do exist and have been documented.[6] In their own unique way, the Snowbird community and other factions of Cherokees are also persisting.

One of the more concise analyses of ethnic group persistence comes from Fredrik Barth, who asserts that ethnic groups can persist despite intense culture contact, absence of geographical isolation, and loss of individual members, characteristics that all apply to the Eastern Cherokees. Intense interethnic relations need not destroy an ethnic group's security and identity, particularly in the case of a group like Snowbird where their federal reservation status legally protects the community from attempts by outside whites to seize health, housing, and financial opportunities guaranteed by the U.S. government. Barth emphasizes that sometimes the total cultural make-up of ethnic groups is not as important for ethnic group persistence as the symbolic ethnic boundaries that set off groups.[7]

Edward Spicer has attempted to discover symbols frequently chosen to act as signals of ethnic identity. He suggests that language, so evident in the Cherokees' case, and homelands, as in the case of Jewish ethnic groups, are the two most important signals, with music, dances, and heroes in a secondary position, all functioning to mark off boundaries.[8] Sioux writer Vine Deloria, Jr., emphasizes that the concept of a homeland is crucial to Native American identity: "Tribal existence has always been predicated upon a land base, a homeland, within which tribal existence could take place. The primary concern of Indian tribes has been the protection of the land to which they are related. Once landless, a people must fall back upon religion, social values, or political power. But with a land base, nationalism in a tribal setting is more possible."[9] Through hardships, the Eastern Cherokees have managed to remain on some of their ancestral lands where traditionalists maintain the Cherokee language. Thus, as Spicer indicates, land and language are crucial symbols in maintaining Eastern Cherokee Indian identity.

In 1973 Snowbird sustained a major political attack on its homeland by the white Indian Tomotla community, and since the 1960s intermarriage with non-speakers of Cherokee (either whites, white Indians, or non-speakers from traditionalist families) has threatened the survival of the language in Snowbird. Snowbird traditionalists, nevertheless, maintain an identity as real Indians despite intense relations with whites and white Indians. A core of cultural traits and practices is maintained as signals for "real Indianness" more intensely in Snowbird than in any other Eastern Cherokee community: the Cherokee language, sung as well as spoken; the concept of a homeland; the Trail of Tears Singing, a real Indian ceremony; native crafts, foods, and jewelry; Indian medicine; a basic Indian value system emphasizing harmony; and fullbloodedness, the latter emphasized by persistent efforts to ally and interact with other fullbloods and Cherokee-language speakers and to marry others with these qualities.

Barth has suggested criteria for ethnic groups' persistence: "Common to all these systems is the principle that ethnic identity implies a series of constraints on the kinds of roles an individual is allowed to play, and the partners he may choose for different kinds of transactions."[10] Those Cherokees who make little effort to limit certain types of interactions with whites and, from the point of view of fullbloods, cross over boundaries separating Indians from non-Indians, become classified as white Indians, people who are viewed as Indians in a legal sense only. Although white Indians usually look more white than Indian, the term is also sometimes applied to very Indian-looking people who fail to act as cultural traditionalists in certain situations. Families who have crossed these boundaries are those who for generations have married whites or other "white Indians"; shown a preference for the English language over Cherokee; permanently left the Cherokee area; elected to practice the Protestant Ethic over the Indian Harmony Ethic, as described by Kupferer, even in dealings with fellow Band members; and/or those who openly identify as white to census-takers, employers, or off-reservation schoolmates (but not to the Band's Enrollment Office).[11] From the fullblood Cherokees' view, the world is a continuum of people ranging from real Indians or fullbloods, to less than fullblood real Indians, to white Indians, to wanna-bees (whites who have no legal status as Indians but who want to be Indians because of possible Indian ancestry), to whites. Real Indians perceive of white Indians as straddling the boundary between red and white, thinking and behaving more like whites than Indians while being legally enrolled members of the Eastern Band in order to gain various economic advantages. Frequently white Indians engage in behavior and transactions quite different from the type in which fullbloods engage. Many fullbloods simply view white Indians as opportunists who wish to have all the advantages of being Indians without enduring any of the prejudices and without being willing to work to make life better for Indians. Whites are often more respected than white Indians or wanna-bees.

All this is not to suggest that traditionalist Snowbird Cherokees never "act like whites." In certain situations they do. Steven Polgar's concept of biculturation has some applicability here.[12] Many traditionalist Indians know white American culture the way they know the English language. Certain situations necessitate the use of English although the speaker may prefer the Cherokee language, just as some situations necessitate white behavior when traditionalist Cherokee behavior may be preferred. Cherokees employed in wage labor, for example, are highly likely to "punch the clock" and conform to white notions of time in the workplace. The same individuals will operate on "Indian time" and arrive "late" when attending a Cherokee function. There are also some situations when traditionalist Cherokees will not "act white" even if such behavior would be advantageous in dealing with whites. It is inconceivable, for example, that a traditionalist would openly criticize a co-worker's job performance even if ordered to do so by his boss. White Indians, by contrast, are perceived as people who consistently "act white" and almost never "act Indian." Acting white only occasionally is, by contrast, analogous to speaking a few words of Spanish without that making one a citizen of Spain.

A pivotal element in the Snowbird community's relations with outsiders is its positive perception of itself as a group of real Indians. This identity has done much to aid the community in controlling its relations with the outside world. The Snowbird community does not correspond to what one textbook on Indians terms "the popular image of the Indians as a broken people uniformly demoralized by feelings of worthlessness and powerlessness."[13] Snowbird Cherokees are an appropriate example of a Native American community that is persisting and adapting with a clearly defined, favorable ethnic identity. While some segments of Cherokee society are indeed being assimilated as the result of intense relations with non-Indians, others, like Snowbird, are persisting with some success despite these conditions.

DISCRIMINATION BY WHITES

Although Snowbird Cherokees do seem to get along better with their non-Indian neighbors than is the case for other Cherokee communities, the group is sometimes subjected to discriminatory practices and demeaning stereotypes. Seldom openly expressed, the derogatory stereotypes picture Indians as lazy, tardy, and financially irresponsible, the latter view leading to the stereotype that Indians accept government handouts.

Anyone who has lived in the Snowbird community must surely realize how absurd such characterizations are. Stereotypes are often even contradictory. For example, whites refer to Indians as welfare cases, supposedly accepting monthly checks from the government, yet the same whites confide with certainty that Indians are wealthy with secret caches of gold and rubies, saved and enlarged for generations. These examples show common, if contradictory, characteristics applied to Cherokees by whites. The stereotypes, even if seldom voiced, are entrenched. A prominent Snowbird man, the late Gaffney Long, told the story of how after his father's death, whites descended on the family property, digging it up and searching for his father's supposed gold. Even though the group left empty-handed, rumors of hordes of wealth have persisted since the pre-removal, gold-rush days. In another case, a white man asserted that a young Indian man's car was a gift of the government. In fact, the young man's uncle had worked very hard, even taking on a second job, in order to save enough money to purchase the automobile for his nephew.

Discriminatory practices are occasionally blatant. Indians in Graham County were largely denied the vote until the late 1940s. Cases of name-calling and fights instigated by disgruntled whites occurred when Cherokee students were integrated into Graham County public schools in the 1950s and 1960s, despite the fact that the school system was and is paid thousands of federal dollars each year for Indian students enrolled in county schools. Apparently, one local factory has made a de facto decision not to hire Indian workers while another was slow to hire more than one or two, despite the fact that 16.7 percent of the adult Indian population is engaged in factory employment—more than in any other one area of full-time employment. Some members of the Cherokee community claimed that a teenage Indian girl lost first place in a school beauty pageant because an influential white did not want an Indian to represent the school. Some whites are also reluctant, though rarely openly hostile, to allow their children to date or marry Indians. The results of a social-distance questionnaire administered in 1974 to all Robbinsville High School students indicate that whites are reluctant to marry Indians or have members of their family marry Indians. The questionnaire found that 65.8 percent of white males and 60.7 percent of white females had problems with the idea of marrying an Indian. In every other category on the questionnaire, however, vastly more whites than not saw nothing wrong in interacting with Indians. In most categories on the questionnaire even larger percentages of Indians were receptive toward interaction with whites, including intermarriage.

DISCRIMINATION BY OTHER CHEROKEES

Snowbird Cherokees are occasionally subject to stereotyping and discriminatory feelings and practices not only by local whites but by other Cherokees. The Snowbird community sometimes feels it is inappropriately treated in its relations with the Qualla Boundary and the Cherokee County Indian community of Tomotla. The political controversy that will be described later in detail is a case in point, and there are other examples. Snowbird is quite far removed from the Qualla Boundary and the services for Indians provided there, such as health care and educational services offered through the recently expanded Indian Health Service Hospital and the modern Bureau of Indian Affairs Cherokee High School. Because Snowbird is not anywhere near the geographical center of the Eastern Cherokee population, and because Snowbird is a traditionalist community, Snowbird people explain that it is doubtful someone from the community will ever again serve the Band in a high official position, such as principal chief or vice chief.

In some ways, therefore, Snowbird feels neglected and omitted from the mainstream of Band activities. Yet the community also feels discriminated against because it is not totally a part of the larger Cherokee group. Many Snowbird athletes playing basketball or football on Graham County school teams have faced real or potential dangers from Indian players on Qualla Boundary school teams who resented Snowbird players' performing for a so-called white school. Former Snowbird athletes cite instances of attempts to foul Snowbird players and of fights after games as evidence of the dislike for them by Boundary teams.

Many of the problems Snowbird has with other Cherokees have developed out of historically old antagonisms between white Indians and fullbloods, rather than from animosities between specific communities. Some white Indians appear to be insecure in their Indianness. Unsuccessful white Indians sometimes blame their lack of accomplishment on their Indianness, although they may neither look nor act typically Indian. Perhaps then, it should not be surprising that according to some in Snowbird, white Indians resent the moderate success of a predominantly fullblood community such as Snowbird. Snowbird's "success" frequently spares the community from derogatory remarks hurled at other fullbloods by some white Indians—terms such as "crazy," "mean," and "dangerous." As long as one of Snowbird's primary identities is being fullblood, however, the community always runs the risk of likewise being categorized in this manner. Since a reasonable amount of intermarriage exists between Snowbird people and other fullbloods who, once married, may choose to live on the Qualla Boundary, many Snowbird individuals are probably subject to such stereotypes even if Snowbird as a community largely avoids the terms. (Twelve percent of all Snowbird residents were born on the Qualla Boundary, and 17.3 percent of all parents of Snowbird residents were born on the Qualla Boundary, indicating the rate of intermarriage between people in the two areas.)

In the case of white Indians in Cherokee County, Gaffney Long told about the troubles he encountered with Tomotla's Indians upon returning from military duty during World War I. Arriving late one night by train in Andrews, near Tomotla, Long hoped to receive a night's lodging with some Indian family before arranging transportation to Snowbird, thirty miles away, the next morning. He knocked on door after door in the Indian community, only to be repeatedly turned away or not have his knocking answered. Finally, he quit trying and well after midnight began the long walk over the Snowbird Mountains, stopping to sleep outdoors along the way. Certain that traditionalist Snowbird households would not treat another Indian so inhospitably, he cited the incident to illustrate how little he thought white Indians care about fullbloods. The perception that Tomotla's white Indians and Snowbird's fullbloods are irreconcilably different has been publically expressed by individuals from both communities.

Snowbird people do have their prejudices, too. Some Snowbird Cherokees describe whites as "drunken," "sexually immoral," "cheating," and "dishonest," just as some whites use derogatory references toward Indians. If some white Indians resent fullblood communities like Snowbird, then it should be emphasized that there are fullbloods who would like to see white Indians lose some of their Indian rights or even their very status as Indians. Snowbird does, however, often have to cope with groups larger and more powerful than itself, a situation in which local whites and the Qualla Boundary Cherokees never find themselves in dealing with Snowbird.

ADAPTATION

Despite its small size, Snowbird is often successful in dealing with these larger groups, whether the situation is a defensive one, such as the political controversy that will be described later, or one in which the community is taking a leadership role, such as the religious ceremony that will also be described later. In the area of employment, for example, the community is quite adept at tapping both tribal and county resources. There is the case of two Indian police deputies who worked for Graham County but were paid by the Eastern Band. There is also an example of a Snowbird woman who was hired by the county school system to teach the Cherokee language but was paid with money funnelled through the Eastern Band. Another Indian, a man, taught at the same school but was paid directly by the county. In the past several years Indians have been employed through Mainstream programs, some by the county's program and some by the Band's. In the 1980s when Snowbird people felt their children were not receiving a fair share of college scholarship money funnelled through tribal government, they founded the Ed Jackson Memorial Scholarship Fund. In 1990 enough money had been earned on the principle to award two small scholarships, one to a Snowbird Cherokee boy and one to a white Graham County girl. Although most Snowbird people seek employment in or near Graham County, the option of commuting to the Qualla Boundary to work in tourist-related enterprises is always open. Some people, particularly women, are employed part-time making baskets and other craft items for sale on the Boundary. Back in 1971 the Band sponsored a small sewing enterprise in Snowbird for local Indians, but unfortunately it was unsuccessful, due presumably to the distance from the community to major transportation routes.

A look at health services available to Snowbird further indicates how divergent sources are tapped by the community. Technically, the Indian Health Service Hospital on the Qualla Boundary is available to the entire Eastern Cherokee population, including the Snowbird community. The hospital, however, is fifty miles from Snowbird. At least two other hospitals offering an equal number or more services are closer to Snowbird, which means the one on the Boundary is not especially convenient and can never be used in real emergencies by the distant Snowbird community. As a result, several procedures have been arranged to upgrade health services for Snowbird. Staff members from the IHS Hospital on the Boundary held a clinic in the community building at Snowbird once a month until the late 1970s, when the Snowbird community built a real health clinic on the banks of Snowbird Creek. Medical staff commuted from the Boundary once or twice a month. In addition, a white-run clinic in Graham County was paid through funds originating on the Boundary to treat Indian patients between the hours of nine and ten in the morning six days a week. (In emergencies the clinic saw Indian patients any time, free of charge to the individual.) Now the Snowbird IHS Clinic has a full-time nurse—Lou Ellen Jones, a fullblood Snowbird Cherokee—and physicians and dentists commute weekly from the Qualla Boundary. Until arrangements were worked out with tribal government, the hospital closest to the Snowbird community in Cherokee County refused to treat Indian patients, telling them to go to their "own hospital" on the Qualla Boundary. Yet the hospital in Cherokee County is a regional facility, financed by three counties including Graham, and is supposed to serve any patient from the three-county area. Since a system of payments by the Eastern Band has been arranged for the hospital, the institution now serves Indian patients. Lou Ellen Jones was employed and paid by the hospital although her training was financially supported through the Band.

When the Snowbird Rescue Squad sought money to purchase a badly needed new ambulance (the old one had broken down while rushing a patient to a hospital), the community argued successfully that the Band should pay part of the cost since Snowbird was not getting as great a benefit out of most health services already provided to Band members. Several people in the Snowbird community took Red Cross courses to become qualified to administer both basic first-aid and cardiopulmonary resuscitation (CPR) and to operate the ambulance. Nevertheless, money is routinely budgeted by the Band to maintain the Cherokee Rescue Squad operating on the Boundary, while the Snowbird Rescue Squad must petition the Band for any funding it receives. Since the Graham County Rescue Squad is available for the local white population, Snowbird's is almost exclusively for the use of the Indian community, although some squad members claim that in an emergency they would certainly transport non-Indians. Without doubt they would serve the non-Indian spouses of Snowbird's people.

In the matter of education Snowbird also exploits every available opportunity. Since the boarding school on the Qualla Boundary closed in the 1950s, Snowbird students have been attending previously all-white public schools in Graham County that receive a subsidy funnelled through the Band for every Indian child enrolled. At times money has also flowed into the public schools to teach Cherokee students who are not fluent in their native tongue. If a student can find lodging with a relative on the Qualla Boundary, he or she may attend Bureau of Indian Affairs schools there. Like other Cherokee students, those from Snowbird who desire post-high school education can often obtain scholarship money. A Snowbird girl studying surveying at a nearby technical school was paid a salary by the Band. Frequently, college students are partially assisted with tuition or transportation costs by the Band or helped in locating scholarships. A Snowbird youth was assisted with various costs of attending college in Kansas, and a Snowbird girl was awarded a scholarship to attend a nearby college.

The Snowbird Head Start Day Care School, which closed in the early 1980s, was the last school in the Snowbird area operated exclusively for Cherokee children. The school handled about two dozen children from age two to age six, assisting them with basic learning skills and ensuring that their English was fluent, while freeing many of their mothers for full-time jobs. Several other Head Start schools still operate on the Boundary, and Snowbird children now attend a Head Start school in Robbinsville with local white children.

Through the schools many Snowbird students have begun participating in previously all-white activities. Nowhere is this more evident than in sports. It was in athletics that the first groups of Indians to attend the public schools proved themselves "worthy" of active participation in a white-dominated world. Although Cherokees constitute only about 5 percent of Graham County's population, they have frequently constituted up to 10 percent of those on teams representing the county's largest high school. Today Cherokees participate not only as players, cheerleaders, band members, and spectators at local athletic events but as coaches as well, with three or four Indian adults instructing various ages of girls and boys on football and basketball teams. In the summer, groups of adults, both white and Indian, form softball teams. Frequently Snowbird men and women each form teams. Because the Indian population is small, Indian team members sometimes invite white friends to play. At one time the Snowbird men's team had four white players and five Indians.

Despite living fifty miles from the main reservation, Snowbird people also participate in Indian activities centered there. During football and basketball season many people from Snowbird travel to the Qualla Boundary to see relatives who play on the high school teams. Probably the most significant activity, however, is the annual Fall Festival. Of fifteen girls competing for the Miss Fall Festival title in 1975, for example, four were from Snowbird, although Snowbird people constitute only about 5 percent of the enrolled members of the Eastern Band of Cherokee Indians. Of nine girls competing for the Miss Cherokee title that same year, one was from Snowbird.

Snowbird people are concerned about their children and use whatever means are at hand to help them. One way is by participating in the Save the Children program operated all over the Eastern Cherokee area and throughout Appalachia and in many Third World countries. Individuals from outside the area sponsor children and send a specified amount of money to a child and his community each year. Tens of thousands of dollars for individual children and thousands for the rescue squad and civic improvements are channeled through Save the Children. In 1971 the Snowbird Community Development Club, which administers the money designated for the community, won a statewide contest for a beautification project partially financed with these funds.

The Qualla Housing Authority is probably the most significant way in recent years that Snowbird has been able to aid itself through its Band affiliation. By 1974 Snowbird had constructed twenty-nine new houses through the initial stages of this program. These constituted 28.4 percent of all occupied houses in Snowbird, and more houses have been built since that time. Some data suggest that Snowbird has been more successful than the average Eastern Cherokee community in obtaining adequate housing. If all Snowbird housing classified by the Eastern Band as either Qualla Housing Authority ("mutual help" housing financed by the Housing Authority), new, good, or improved are grouped together, they constitute 56.8 percent of all occupied houses in Snowbird. In other words, no more than 43.2 percent of Snowbird housing could be classified as substandard by 1974, while during a comparable time period for the Eastern Band as a whole, nearly 60 percent of housing was substandard.[14] Certainly the community's influence in Tribal Council helped secure the new housing. Built by communal labor, the houses have upgraded the living standard of many. Another matter relating to housing further reveals the efforts of Snowbird to use every means available to help itself.

One family with an irresponsible household head was unable to meet the qualifications for a new house through the housing authority. Several members of the community were convinced a way had to be found to assist the family, and on a particularly cold, rainy day the Band-employed community health representative, William Jackson, brought some members of tribal government to visit the cold, leaking, overcrowded house. Thereafter, funds were forthcoming to purchase supplies and hire Snowbird men to build a new house for the family.

Thus, Snowbird effectively manipulates the system to help itself, whether in the case of employment, health services, education, or housing. One means by which Snowbird manages to survive as well as it does is through active political involvement, both in Band and county government. Until recently Snowbird was guaranteed two of the twelve seats in tribal council, and today the community still virtually controls one. Active participation in county politics includes the fact that two Snowbird men have held the position of vice president of the county Democratic Party and others have served on precinct committees. One Snowbird man has considered running for a county commissioner's seat and has been appointed to a four-county advisory board on regional problems.

Snowbird knows well how to use its resources, whether obtained through the Eastern Band, Graham County, or through the strength and fortitude of its own people. The *gadugi* may no longer exist in Snowbird as a formal cooperative organization, but in the sense that the word means "working together," *gadugi* is still alive. During one typical winter a former *gadugi* captain, Mason Ledford, and the community health representative, William Jackson, spent much of their free time cutting firewood for persons unable to cut their own. Without their assistance several people would have been without heat or a means for cooking. In 1974 the men made an unsuccessful effort to obtain Community Action Program funds to support their work, again indicating Snowbird people's awareness about diverse resources likely to be available to help the community. One reason for the demise of the formal *gadugi*, or free labor company, is that salaries have become available to pay individuals such as the community health representative, to do work that was once done by voluntary communal labor.

The Snowbird Funeral Association that, like similar groups elsewhere on the Eastern Cherokee reservation, once formed part of the *gadugi* organization is now part of the Snowbird Community Development Club. Elsewhere in the Eastern Cherokee area the *gadugi* and the community clubs have remained separate, the former attracting fullbloods and the latter white Indians. In Snowbird, however, many of the functions and members of the *gadugi* seem to have been absorbed into the community club where they continue to survive and work. During the summer the club holds Saturday night bingo games and hot dog suppers which alternate between benefiting the funeral association and the rescue squad. People from every faction of the community support the activities, realizing that inevitably they or their relatives will benefit from either or both of the services supported in this manner. The system works like an insurance program with everyone paying larger than average sums of money for a Saturday's entertainment, realizing that from their pooling of resources future major expenses will be covered for each family.

The efforts of Snowbird to help itself are sometimes quite tangible, such as the Sunday school addition to Buffalo Baptist Church in the 1970s. With money from the church treasury and the volunteer labor of its members, the new structure was gradually built. In a similar spirit Little Snowbird Baptist Church built a children's playground in the 1980s with donations from an Atlanta church and volunteer labor from the Snowbird community. Even members of other churches pitched in to build the Church of the Lamb on tribal land.

Other areas of community concern are more intangible. Since 1972 when the final stages of the Band's land claims settlement with the federal government began, some Snowbird people talked about using a portion of the money they expected to gain to buy more reservation land for Cherokees who now live on non-Indian land. Such concern for the welfare of others in the group is characteristic of the Snowbird community. In fact, although the Eastern Band as a whole finally voted for a straight per capita division of the Indian Claims Commission money, Snowbird supported a position that would have put the money to work on group projects, possibly investing the money and using the interest to supplement the incomes of the elderly and provide scholarship money for students. The recently developed Ed Jackson Memorial Scholarship Fund works in a similar fashion to aid college-bound students from the Snowbird area.

SUCCESSFUL IMAGE

In addition to being adaptive, the community possesses a positive image of itself. It refers to whites almost exclusively as "non-Indians," a term categorizing whites as outsiders to the primary Indian group, rather than viewing Indians as the group omitted from the mainstream. Likewise, a minister who preached in a local church enjoyed referring to Cherokee as an "American language" and English as a "foreign language," much to the delight of the congregation. This view is expressed whether or not whites are present at the church service.

The same minister also enjoyed working references to Cherokee traditions into his impromptu sermons. On one occasion he lingered on traditional Cherokee attitudes toward death and funerals, emphasizing that for three days after attending a funeral a participant was considered "contaminated" and would stay home as much as possible, resting to "recover" from the contamination. Such traditions were openly discussed in that church, again even in the presence of whites.

In other ways members of the Snowbird community also characterize themselves favorably. At one community club meeting the notion was expressed that in jobs relating to Indian concerns Indians should obtain the positions if they were equally or better qualified than non-Indians. That many qualified Indians were available was also mentioned.

On another occasion, after a reported suicide on the main reservation, a young Snowbird man stated that although a high suicide rate existed on the Qualla Boundary that kind of thing was rare in Snowbird. He realized that the suicide rate on the Boundary was probably higher than for surrounding white communities but thought Snowbird's was less than either of those groups. Again the image emerges of Snowbird as a community which assumes it can cope with its problems.

Snowbird people have a sense of their history as unique and noble. In the 1980s Shirley Oswalt was among some Snowbird people who formed the Junaluska Society to perpetuate the memory of the famous Cherokee leader buried in Graham County. The society is in the process of raising funds to purchase Junaluska's grave site and return it to Indian control. The society would also like to develop school courses on Cherokee heritage. Shirley Oswalt, a fluent Cherokee-language speaker, has recently learned to read and write in the Cherokee syllabary as part of that effort.

Probably nowhere does the favorable and well-adjusted image Snowbird has of itself come across more clearly than in Snowbird children's drawings. Draw-a-person tests were given to nine Indian Head Start children; ten first- and second-graders in a Cherokee-language class in a Graham County elementary school, all Indians; a sixth-grade class in a Graham County elementary school, comprising 29 whites and three Indians; dozens of Indian students on the Qualla Boundary; and other selected Snowbird children.

It is noteworthy that all three of the Indian students enrolled in the Graham County sixth-grade class drew Indians when asked to draw "a person." According to Wayne Dennis, members of a minority ethnic group tend to draw someone representing the dominant group if the minority group has a low opinion of itself.[15] Since all the Indian children in that class drew Indians, the results of the test tend to indicate that Snowbird Cherokees have a satisfactory image of themselves. What is also significant is that four white sixth-grade students likewise drew Indians when asked to draw "a person." The four white students who drew an Indian and one of the three Indian students drew a real person, either an Indian student in the class or the instructor, Gilliam Jackson, who was then the only fully employed Indian teacher in the Graham County schools. The two other drawings by Indians are both of idealized Indian-looking people. One of the four white students who chose an Indian as his subject drew a caricature of his best friend, an Indian. Many of the drawings by white students were of idealized whites; many were of beautiful blonde women with large red lips, a subject frequently chosen by white girls in the class. One white boy drew a "hillbilly," caricaturing his own ethnic group, and it is interesting to compare this drawing to one of the Indian students' drawings caricaturing his own ethnic group by presenting an Indian wearing a feathered headdress. A few of the Snowbird Cherokee girls drew beautiful dark-haired women with braids. It is interesting that the Qualla Boundary Indian students seldom drew Indians and never as an idealized type.

CHEROKEE LANGUAGE

Despite Snowbird's intense interaction with other groups of people, which has often won respect for the community, the community consciously clings to a core group of traditionalist Cherokee traits. Nowhere is this more obvious than with the Cherokee language. Although by the mid-1970s, Cherokee as the language spoken by entire households was only used by about half the community and has continued to decline as a household language, 74.5 percent of Snowbird residents over the age of eighteen, including non-Indian spouses, spoke fluent Cherokee.

The Cherokee language is routinely used in the three oldest Snowbird churches; one of them, Little Snowbird, uses it almost exclusively. That church has regularly invited Cherokee-speaking ministers from Oklahoma and fullblood areas of the Qualla Boundary to come preach in the Cherokee language. The Snowbird Cherokee writer Gilliam Jackson singles out the churches as one of the main institutions for preserving the language.[16] Likewise, the language is spoken throughout community club meetings with English used only for non-Cherokee-language speakers who occasionally attend. Most of the people speaking Cherokee in these contexts are also fluent English speakers, so they speak Cherokee by choice in these settings. There are also whole families who speak English but consciously use Cherokee in the home to perpetuate the Indian language, a few of them even giving their children Indian as well as English names. Little compromise is made in these settings with those who speak English only, with the result that some English-speaking Snowbird residents are discouraged, for example, from attending community club meetings. One middle-aged woman, a lifelong resident of Snowbird who does not speak Cherokee, confided she had not known that another lifelong resident spoke fluent English, so reluctant was the other woman to speak English to other Indians. I only discovered that Ella Jackson, a good friend and one of my key informants, spoke English when we were first alone together and there was no one else to translate her Cherokee. All of the previous arrangements for me to live in her old house had taken place with her brother, Ned Long, translating.

Many of those in Snowbird who do not speak Cherokee are non-

Indians, or Qualla Boundary Cherokees, or the children of either of those types of people. In fact, there are people who worry that intermarriage with non-Indians or white Indians will not only change the physical appearance of Snowbird's population but will cause the Cherokee language to die out. Gilliam Jackson, Ella's son, writes, "What is even sadder is that many people know the language but choose not to use it."[17] When extra money became available to finance new educational programs in the public schools for Cherokee children, however, Snowbird parents meeting with school officials decided to use the money to have the Cherokee language taught, a situation that became a reality within a year's time. Thus, Snowbird took assertive action toward correcting a condition that met with community disapproval. It is significant that Eidheim has specifically singled out the teaching of native language and history in the schools as key issues in the Lappish Movement, a Norwegian phenomenon that shares many common elements with the Native American identity movement in the United States and Canada. Also, as has been pointed out, Spicer singles out language as a major symbol in maintaining ethnic identity.[18]

CRAFTS

Recently there have been attempts to teach craft skills in the same formal manner in which the Cherokee language has been taught. A continuing education program has taught craft skills at Snowbird Tech, a one-room building near the local BIA representative's home, for several years. Crafts such as basketmaking and beadworking have been taught in the public school system with funds for Indian education. There are several older women in the community who are skilled in basketmaking. They gather and process native basketmaking materials, such as walnut, bloodroot, and yellowroot stains and split oak, cane, and honeysuckle vines, just as they continue to gather ginseng (*Panax quinquefolium*), a medicinal plant, and ramps (*Allium tricoccum*), a wild bulbous food related to the onion.

MYTHS AND INDIAN DOCTORS

Occasionally, even the old Cherokee myths play a part in the lives of Snowbird people. During a sermon at Buffalo Baptist Church, an Indian minister referred favorably to the myth "The Origin of Disease and Medicine."[19] The myth, which explains the origin of conjuring, relates that human overpopulation became so intense that the animals in revenge for being crowded off their land sent diseases to afflict mankind. The plants, however, took pity on people, and each offered to be a cure for one disease. According to the myth, it is simply up to conjurors ("Indian doctors") to discover which plant is the remedy for each disease. Instead of counterposing Cherokee mythology and Christian doctrine, the minister considered the two compatible. In the minister's reinterpretation of the myth only Jesus can heal illness, accomplishing His purpose through physicians or "conjure men," whose duty it is to locate the plant or herb which will cure a particular disease. The same minister occasionally referred to himself jokingly as a "conjure man," "witch doctor," or "booger."

Some Indian doctors, or conjurors, continue to practice their knowledge in the Snowbird community. Raymond Fogelson has made a distinction between conjurors, specialists in medicine who combine ceremonies with curing, and mere herbalists, who dispense herbs to cure disease but rarely know accompanying ceremonies.[20] Both categories are said to "doctor" patients, although in Snowbird only a few genuine conjurors still practice. Both men and women, mostly older people, do conjuring in Snowbird, curing everything from an unattractive naval to an infant's inability to drink milk to a severe burn. More ordinary ailments, such as headaches, sore throats, and insomnia, are also treated. In most cases dissatisfaction with initial treatment by a white physician prompts visits to an Indian doctor. Some Indian doctors work on whites as well as Indians, and some whites also practice herbal medicine. Conjuring is not something counterposed to modern medicine but as in the case of Cherokee mythology and Christianity, both are used in combination. One Indian doctor in Snowbird is also a Christian minister, and another is a former councilmember. In contrast to Fogelson's findings on the Qualla Boundary, Snowbird does not appear to regard Indian doctors as individuals "unable to compete for the rewards offered by white culture" thus turning to conjuring to compensate for low self-esteem.[21]

HARMONY ETHIC

Perhaps the most significant aspects of Snowbird's conservative attitude toward Cherokee traits are the elements of the Harmony Ethic persisting in the community.[22] No more obvious example of the Harmony Ethic can be cited than the way generosity manifests itself via housing. With the proliferation of new houses in Snowbird due to the mutual-help housing program, several older but adequate houses were available to be rented out when I began my fieldwork. Yet probably not one of these houses was used in this manner. Instead they were made available to relatives or friends to live in as long as necessary, for several years or more, entirely rent-free. In the summer of 1990 Shirley Oswalt and I counted up all the people who had benefited from living for a time in her parents' old house, the two of us included. The house has since burned down but not before providing shelter to dozens of people. One of the worst things that can be said about a traditionalist Cherokee is that he is stingy. Robert Daniels has observed a similar situation among traditional Oglala Sioux: "To the whites a nuclear family should be economically self-sufficient and should operate on a budget of cash provided by the labor of the 'man of the family.' . . . To the Oglalas, who hold on to the community generosity patterns and take part in give-away ceremonies, the whites appear stingy and disloyal even to their own relatives."[23]

Even traditionalist Cherokees are not naive and maladaptive in their generosity, however. A young Snowbird man, who frequently assists people in the community, once refused to help a woman from Snowbird whose car had broken down on the road, even when she attempted to flag him down. He explained that since she never helps anyone else in the community, people were now unwilling to assist her. Daniels writes about similar cases among the Oglala: "Those individuals who continually refuse to adjust to the group's attitudes are excluded in order to preserve what harmony exists. Even in the case of their very close relatives, traditional Oglalas will regretfully 'give up on them.' There is no sense in being generous and sociable toward a person who does not share one's appreciation of such good deeds."[24]

The *gadugi*, or free labor company, which operated as a source of communal labor until about forty years ago, supposedly never elected officers but chose its captain and other leaders by group consensus, another example of an effort to maintain harmony. Many of the functions of the *gadugi* have now been absorbed into the community club where officers are formally elected but with much joking among those present and great shows of modesty by those elected to demonstrate everyone's noncompetitiveness. Those who do seek an excessive number of positions in the community are derided for "putting themselves over everyone."

Harmony Ethic behavior can best be understood by comparing it to aspects of typical white behavior. At a white church near Snowbird the occasion of electing new deacons prompted one prominent church member to urge other members to point out openly any behavior considered wrong or sinful in another individual. Cherokee churches do not urge such behavior, and if they did, it is doubtful whether an Indian would walk up to another individual and tell him point blank what was wrong about his behavior. That would be too aggressive.

Wax has analyzed assertiveness among traditionalist Western Cherokees in Oklahoma and sees similarities with the Eastern Band. He is considering the effects of formal education on Cherokee children when he writes:

> Only when the self becomes subordinated, as when the individual is the representative of a band of his fellows, can the child comfortably perform in solo fashion before an audience. In the arithmetic race between two teams of pupils, where members of each team work successively at the board in competition with the other to complete the problem most rapidly, Cherokee derive great satisfaction. Victory manifests the competency of the team, and the individual performs for the service of the group. In contrast, during normal class work, individual Cherokee go most reluctantly to the board to work alone and before the observant gaze of their fellows.[25]

What Wax is suggesting is that assertiveness is acceptable behavior to traditionalist Cherokees if it is done for the good of the group, a Harmony Ethic trait. If such behavior is done for the advancement of the individual alone, it is unacceptable. Therefore, there are instances of assertiveness that are typical of "real Indian" behavior.

RELATIONS WITH THE OUTSIDE WORLD

Some of Snowbird's activities, church services, the community club, rescue squad, and funeral association, are rarely broader than the community itself. Other activities involve cooperation with other Eastern Cherokee communities. These include participation in Tribal Council and the dealings with the Indian Claims Commission. Still others involve working with non-Indians, for example, county government, the monthly Sunday church singings, school sports, and the adult softball teams. Others, the Trail of Tears Singing, health and educational services, and employment opportunities, involve the community with both Western and other Eastern Cherokees and non-Indians. Some activities even involve the community with Indians other than Cherokees: the Fall Festival, the North Carolina Commission on Indian Affairs, and the organization of United Southeastern Tribes. Concerning the United Southeastern Tribes, the Sioux Indian writer Vine Deloria, Jr., says:

> The federal tribes of the southeastern United States, always separated by distance and ideology, recently moved in the direction of a southeastern coalition of tribes. The Choctaws of Mississippi and the Seminoles and the Miccosukees of Florida recently banded together with the Eastern Band of Cherokees of North Carolina to form an intertribal council to work specifically on their problems.
>
> As federal policies change and become clarified, there is little doubt that the southeastern United States will experience a great Indian revival, bringing the focus in Indian Affairs to philosophy rather than program considerations.[26]

The Eastern Cherokees' isolation from other Indians is decreasing. In the case of intermarriage, for example, there are Snowbird people wed to "real" and white Indians, non-Indians, and even non-Cherokee Indians.

"REAL INDIAN" IDENTITY

Despite interaction with all these groups and the disappearance or decline of some traditional Cherokee traits, Snowbird maintains a core identity as a "real Indian" community. Eleanor Leacock's observations on what makes Indians "real Indians" are illuminating: "Indians have played a role in American history, and . . . they still have a role to play, neither as 'museum pieces' nor as individuals lost in the 'melting pot,' but as Indians of the twentieth century. Indian traditions and experiences have neither fossilized nor disappeared; Indian ways of today are not those of centuries ago, but they are nonetheless Indian. Indian cultural traditions have continued to grow and change, and there has been constant integration of innovations into characteristically Indian ways and Indian views."[27] Snowbird perceives that this core identity need not exclude other roles for itself and that adaptation is not equivalent to assimilation. Some Snowbird residents clearly articulate their determination that Cherokee identity must be maintained, as the Snowbird Cherokee writer

Gilliam Jackson states in his article, "Cultural Identity for the Modern Cherokees":

> Young Indians today are involved in a struggle against seemingly insurmountable odds. That struggle is to retain our Indian identity in a world increasingly dominated by Anglos and Anglo ways. My generation is at a watershed; we are nearing the point of no return. If our Indianness is to be preserved, if we are to retain our pride in what we have been and what we are and can be today, we must become active in the struggle against the loss of our Indian heritage and our Indian identity. . . . Obviously we Cherokees cannot return completely to our traditional way of life. What we can do is affirm the value of our Indianness and stop trying to imitate the white man in all ways. By being ourselves and by preserving some of the ways of our ancestors that help us retain our Indian identity, we can save our Indian communities where people can still live in peace with their environment and with their fellow men.[28]

An article in the *Cherokee One Feather* further illustrates the growing Cherokee ethnic identity:

> Traditional Cherokee songs and dances are being taught to the elementary grades [on the Qualla Boundary]. . . . It's important for the children to know about their heritage so they can identify themselves as Cherokees. . . . We, as parents and teachers, should instill in the minds of our Indian children that the Indian is proud, proud of his heritage and ancestry and at the same time enlighten the white man that we were not savage, warlike, barbarious and the numerous derogatory terms and names given us. . . . The Eastern Cherokee are especially proud of their ancestors who refused to be moved by the land and gold hungry whites in the 1830's and today we can still hold our heads high in pride regardless of the treatment given our ancestors on the "Trail of Tears."[29]

Thus, despite vast changes in Cherokee culture and an identification as Americans, today Eastern Cherokees perceive of themselves as the cultural, as well as the genealogical, descendants of previous generations of Cherokee Indians. A distinct ethnic identity as "real Indians" persists, especially in Snowbird.

3

A Political Controversy

Overleaf: Ned Long was at the heart of the 1973 political controversy. Snowbird council members suggested that Indian Claims money be invested and used for some group purpose.
Photo by Ken Murray, 1990.

Two specific events, or situations, observed during the course of fieldwork can be used as microcosms of nearly every type of identity the Snowbird Cherokee community assumes in its relations with other groups of people. One of the events presents the community in a joyous, confident mood as organizers and leaders of a religious ceremony. The other, which will be described first, presents the community in a strategic, defensive pose as participants in a crucial political controversy. It is exactly the type of situation, a political dispute, which J. van Velsen singles out as particularly appropriate for the extended-case method, or situational analysis, which will be used here.

The detailed description of a particular situation, when presented effectively, does more than merely illustrate some point. It is a demonstration in microcosm of the functioning of a key aspect of the society. Situational analysis deemphasizes impressions in favor of facts and allows the reader, removed from the fieldwork situation, to develop a visual image of exactly how particular aspects of a society function. As van Velsen explains: "By this method the ethnographer not only presents the reader with abstractions and inferences from his field material but also provides some of the material itself. This puts the reader in a better position to evaluate the ethnographer's analysis not only on the basis of the internal consistency of the argument, but also by comparing the ethnographic data with the inferences drawn from them."[1] By drawing on actual field notes and acknowledging the personal, as well as professional, role of the ethnographer, the reader is put directly in touch with the circumstances of a particular case representative of the culture in question.

I am inspired in applying the situational analysis method to the Snowbird Cherokees by Max Gluckman's pioneering study of the Zulu used to analyze black-white relations in South Africa.[2] Modern British social anthropologists like Gluckman have strived to discover methods of presenting the social organization of cultures as a *process* rather than as rigid *structures.* It is an attempt to depart from the methods of the first part of this century which inadvertently resulted in the presentation of Third and Fourth World peoples as unchanging and maladaptive. The Snowbird Cherokees are, for example, traditionalists and yet they constantly implement adaptive strategies in their adjustment to the larger, industrialized world.

Gluckman has emphasized that conflict, especially political conflict, exists in every society and is a by-product of any ongoing process of adaptivity. Fredrik Barth has focused on the dilemmas and difficult choices individuals and societies confront in the process of being adaptive.[3] Barth has also pointed out the necessity of an approach emphasizing process in the study of ethnicity and ethnic relations.[4]

The application of situational analysis in presenting the Snowbird Cherokee data is a sincere attempt to emphasize the adaptive process.

THE FIELD SETTING

I began a yearlong stay with the Snowbird Cherokees in the spring of 1973. Snowbird attracted my interest for two reasons. First, everyone from James Mooney to John Gulick had suggested someone should study this academically neglected community. Second, the community seemed to have many characteristics of a traditionalist community, including large percentages of fullbloods and Cherokee-language speakers, and yet it also seemed modern in its adaptations.

I had had some brief contact with the community in 1971 when, as part of my M.A. thesis research on Cherokee education, I spent a couple of days doing observations at the Snowbird Head Start School. The first day that I drove from the main reservation to Snowbird I fell in love with the area's natural beauty. The drive along the Nantahala Gorge and then Snowbird Creek is truly lovely. The mountains, covered with dark virgin forests, rise sharply from the narrow valleys. Snowbird Creek is swift and clear, and the road follows its every twist and curve.

New houses, built with loans secured by tribal government, were interspersed with old ramshackle cabins. At the time many older homes were vacant because the former residents had only recently built their new homes. Early in the spring of 1973 when I made three successive trips to Snowbird to secure housing, I mistakenly assumed it would be easy to find an older vacant house to rent. But only nearby whites seemed interested in renting to me. Why, I wondered, would not the Indians?

One of the first families I made contact with on those brief trips was the Longs, kinsmen of James Mooney's famous informant, Will West Long. Ned Long was, at the time, one of two members of Tribal Council from Snowbird. His father, Gaffney Long, had been a trusted adviser to several Eastern Cherokee chiefs during the first half of this century. I sought Ned out to ask permission to do fieldwork in Snowbird. Like most Cherokees, he seemed to find it mildly amusing that I assumed anyone had the power to grant or deny me such permission. But he did invite me into his home, and I discovered that his wife Shirley and I had met earlier at the Head Start School where she worked. Ned is fullblood Cherokee, a member of the Deer Clan. Shirley is white. Theirs was one of the first interracial marriages in Snowbird. They lived in a new home, overlooking Santeetlah Lake, with their four children, Patricia, Johnny, Ned, and Brenda. The Longs were kind enough to provide me with sleeping quarters and hearty meals which always included plenty of beans and cornbread.

Finally, on my last pre-fieldwork trip, Ned introduced me to his sister, Ella Long Jackson. She and her husband Ed had an old home near where her parents lived, and Ned suggested she might let me stay there. We met Ella at the old house. Ella spoke Cherokee, and Ned translated. I learned much later that Ella speaks fluent English. After we talked for awhile, Ned announced that the house was mine. I inquired about the amount of rent and was told there would be no rent. The house was mine as long as I needed it. My only stated obligation was to care for Hobo, the old dog who "came with the house." Later I learned to reciprocate in other ways, too, mostly by looking in on Ella and Ned's aged parents, Gaffney and Susie Long, who lived just up the mountain from Ella's old house.

I got the house for free, I later realized, because I seemed a decent person in need. Friends, even new ones, and kinsmen should be shared with. It would be wrong to be stingy enough to charge rent and make a profit off someone's needs, especially so basic a need as housing.

Ella and Ed have seven children—William, Lou Ellen, Gilliam, Jacob, Shirley, Ethel, and Esther. They and their spouses and children, along with the Longs, became my key informants.

The Longs and Jacksons are traditionalist and yet adaptive people. At the time they worked in factories, went to school, two were in teaching, one was a nurse, another a community health representative, and so on. All were active in tribal government and the Snowbird Community Club, as well as local county affairs. Yet, for the most part, they spoke the Cherokee language and subscribed to the traditional Harmony Ethic that required a Snowbird house to be shared rather than rented. I truly believe no other Eastern Cherokee community is so uniformly traditionalist and representative of Cherokee culture.

It was therefore a shock when I learned that Snowbird's representation in Tribal Council was threatened and that the two Snowbird incumbent councilmembers, Ned Long and Mose Wachacha, might not be re-elected.

THE SIGNIFICANCE OF THE SITUATION

The political event described below developed out of what future anthropologists and historians of the Cherokees may evaluate as the most significant biennial election ever held for Tribal Council. That is clearly how I evaluate the situation. It was the election held on Thursday, September 6, 1973. At that time Tribal Council had twelve representatives of equal voting power, each elected for a two-year term. Each of the twelve councilmembers' votes was weighted the same (and not, as now, proportionate to the number of constituents a councilmember represents). Cherokee lands then and now are divided into six townships: Yellow Hill (Cherokee proper), Birdtown, Painttown, Wolfetown, Big Cove, and Cheoah, each electing two councilmembers. In 1973 Cheoah was equated with the Snowbird community.

There have been three historical events that have reoriented the Cherokees as regards cultural persistence and the process of change. The first happened at the end of the eighteenth and beginning of the nineteenth century. The second occurred almost one hundred years later at the end of the nineteenth century. The third is happening now at the end of the twentieth century. I believe the 1973 political controversy between the real Indian Snowbird community and the white Indian Tomotla community is at the heart of this third reorientation. I have chosen to apply situational analysis to the 1973 case, not because I do not have any more recent or better example, but because that controversy has major historical significance. If I had not been in residence on the North Carolina reservation to observe the dispute, I would have to report on it secondhand.

At the close of the eighteenth century "progressive" factions of Cherokees embarked on a program of accommodation as an adaptive strategy. Not that many years before, the entire Cherokee Nation had been populated by traditionalist fullbloods. But as white Indians pushed through their political, economic, educational, and religious changes in a vain attempt to avoid removal by convincing white Americans the Cherokees

were not savages, they factionalized the Cherokee Nation. From Tomotla to New Echota, mixedbloods carried the day. Across the Snowbird
Mountains communities like Cheoah and Kituhwa, modern-day Snowbird and Qualla, looked to Yonaguska and other Cherokee leaders who
spoke eloquently about preserving Cherokee traditions.

When the grand experiment failed in the removal of 1838, traditionalists were left behind more frequently than progressives. Whites, after
all, had been more interested in Cherokee land (the progressives' land
was good for farming and rich in gold) than in civilizing the Cherokees.
The Eastern Band of Cherokee Indians started off as a nearly homogeneous fullblood society.

At the end of the nineteenth century, whites claiming minimal Cherokee blood degree flooded onto the main Eastern Cherokee reservation,
the Qualla Boundary, hoping to obtain private ownership of sections of
Cherokee land under federal policies like allotment. Once again upheaval
and change disrupted Cherokee society. Intermarriage and the introduction of white American formal education put the main body of Eastern
Cherokees in the same position as the Cherokee Nation a century before. Escaping this white onslaught was the tiny, traditionalist Snowbird
community on reservation lands fifty miles away. On the main reservation, by contrast, soon the best bottomlands were in the hands of white
Indians.

For the last century the federal reservation status of the Eastern
Cherokee lands has offered protection from a further mass white onslaught. In fact, traditionalists typically feel more threatened economically and politically by white Indians than by whites. Whites, unlike
white Indians, cannot share in tribal lands, land claims money, tribal
bingo profits, low-cost housing, or any of a number of benefits available to tribal members. Every two years when the elections for Tribal
Council are held, political factions develop based on blood degree.

In 1973 Snowbird survived as a bastion of traditionalism, the only
politically independent township which always sent two real Indians to
Tribal Council. The Cherokees were once an independent nation of traditionalists. By the end of the eighteenth century it was factionalizing.
The removal created a new Eastern Cherokee tribe peopled by traditionalists. By the end of the nineteenth century, the Eastern Cherokees
were factionalized. In 1973 the last remaining politically independent
community of real Indians, Snowbird, was factionalized and its econ-

omy threatened when the white Indian community of Tomotla sought to consolidate its and Snowbird's lands into a single political township.

Coupled with the integration of Snowbird children into the previously all-white Graham County public schools and the increasing rates of intermarriage between Snowbird traditionalists and either non-Indians or non-Cherokee-language speakers, the political conflict with Tomotla has left the Snowbird community at a cultural watershed here at the end of the twentieth century. Some doubt that the Cherokee language and other traditions can survive. Nevertheless, Snowbird remains the Eastern Cherokee community with the highest percentages of Cherokee-language speakers in every age category and highest percentage of full-bloods. If the Cherokee language survives at all outside of Oklahoma, it will survive in Snowbird.

THE SITUATION

It was already late August of 1973 when I realized that for Snowbird the tribal election would be anything but a simple procedure for returning two incumbents to council. On August 27, I heard rumors about a plot, originating from unknown sources, to eliminate one of the local incumbents from the council race by luring him to run for vice chief, a position he supposedly could not win. On several occasions I learned about impromptu, clandestine, political gatherings of traditionalists in the Snowbird community and on the main reservation, the Qualla Boundary, but never before those gatherings actually occurred. Gulick refers to such political groups composed largely of fullbloods as the "Qualla Group."[5]

Finally, I learned from Councilmember Ned Long the nature of the political controversy: the white Indian Cherokee community of Tomotla in Cherokee County would make an attempt to seize the two Cheoah Township council seats held by the real Indian Cherokee community of Snowbird in Graham County. I had already learned that in 1971 a Tomotla man had been disqualified, due to Snowbird's efforts, from running for a Cheoah Township council seat. In 1973 the Cherokee County community was better organized, and the Tomotla Community Club nominated two candidates, Albert Martin and Bailey Coleman, to run for the Cheoah council seats against the two incumbents, Ned Long and Mose Wachacha, supported by the Snowbird Community Club. Another

Tomotla man, the same who had been disqualified in 1971, ran independently.

Like John Gulick, and everyone else who has studied the North Carolina Cherokees, I initially assumed that the term "Cheoah Township" was synonymous with "Snowbird community" and that Cherokee County Cherokees lived on "scattered tracts" that are "not organized as a township"; i.e., that Tomotla Cherokees were legally, but not politically, tied to the Eastern Band of Cherokee Indians.[6] Apparently it has only been since Gulick's fieldwork in the 1950s that Tomotla Cherokees have expressed an interest in tribal politics. In fact, the wording of the 1897 amendment of the 1889 Cherokee Charter presents the view that "Cheoah" is "Snowbird": "from Cheoah settlement, Graham County, 2 members" shall come.[7]

The 1897 amendment provides for the election of twelve councilmembers, two from each of the six reservation townships. The phrase "Tomotla community" does not appear in the Charter or amendment, and Cherokee County is not described as part of any of the six political townships. It was by invoking the Charter that Snowbird successfully prevented a Tomotla man from running for a Cheoah council seat in 1971. In the summer of 1973 Tomotla decided to clarify its ambiguous position in the Eastern Band of Cherokee Indians by running candidates for council.

The Eastern Cherokees' Tribal Council has a considerable amount of political power over the reservation and is analogous to a city council, a county's board of commissioners, or even a state's legislative branch of government. It passes rules and ordinances to be enforced by the executive branch of tribal government, the Principal Chief and Vice Chief. Council can, for example, appropriate or control money for everything from the Band's police force to a craft cooperative to a health center to a housing authority. In 1990 through the Cherokee Children's Home and Cherokee Boys Club as administrators, Tribal Council took over control of the schools on the Qualla Boundary from the Bureau of Indian Affairs. Federal funds for schools will be administrated through grants. Council can pass ordinances on the sale of alcohol, the quality of crafts sold in tourist shops on the reservation, or how many fishing licenses will be issued to tourists. There is, however, still some confusion over where council's authority ends and the authority of the counties, state, or federal government begins. (The ambiguity may even allow council to do some things it could not if the limits of its authority were sharply defined.) Besides functioning as the legislative branch of tribal government, Tribal Council also often functions as the judicial branch, either directly, particularly in rendering decisions in controversies over land ownership, or indirectly, through its magistrate who renders decisions in civil, probate, and misdemeanor cases. Tribal Council can have direct control over important matters like how many new houses a community will get, whether a community will get a new ambulance, which family will win a land dispute, and whether new jobs will be created. Access to the authority of council is thus important to Eastern Cherokee communities like Snowbird and Tomotla.

I have continued to hear varying estimates of the Cherokee County Indian population. The U.S. Census Bureau listed 71 Indians in Cherokee County in 1970. By 1980 the Census listed 189, for a phenomenal growth rate of 166.2 percent. The estimate I heard most frequently in the days before the election in 1973 was from some Snowbird residents who guessed the figure was over 500, as compared with about 320 in Graham County at the time of the controversy.

Some Snowbird residents, when interviewed before and after the election, often referred to Cherokee County Indians as white Indians or "five-dollar Indians," claiming that Tomotla people do not physically appear to be Indian because their ancestors were whites who bribed census takers to be included on Band rolls. Harriet Kupferer writes that the term, "five-dollar Indian," is also used in the same derogatory way on the main reservation to refer to minimal-blood-degree Cherokees.[8] Apparently from the 1880s well into the twentieth century, some whites have indeed managed to get their names on Cherokee enrollments, although there is no firm data to suggest whether the number of whites having done this was small, or quite large, as contemporary fullbloods suspect.

Realizing the threat from Cherokee County, the Snowbird Community Club strategically chose to nominate only their two incumbents in 1973, as opposed to 1971 when six Snowbird people ran. In addition, no one ran independently from Snowbird. The Snowbird Club also paid the two incumbents' $25 qualifying fees. During the time between which each community club made its nominations and the election, Tomotla representatives offered to split the two council seats, with Snowbird controlling one and Tomotla the other. The two incumbent Snowbird councilmembers rejected the offer, probably assuming that simply invoking the 1897 Cherokee Charter amendment would disqualify any Tomotla candidates, since that very strategy had worked successfully for Snowbird in the 1971 election.

On the Sunday before the election, as the congregation from one of Snowbird's churches, Buffalo Baptist, emptied into the parking area, I noticed Ned Long busily chatting politics with several people and urging them to vote on Thursday. Monday I offered to drive voters to the polls and was told there were a few fullbloods in Cherokee County sympathetic to Snowbird's cause and in need of rides, but that I might be physically endangering myself to help in that way.

I also learned that there were those in Snowbird sympathetic to Tomotla's cause when I discovered that one of the Tomotla candidates, Albert Martin, was married to a Snowbird woman and had in-laws living in Snowbird. His in-laws, the Smokers, as it turned out, had also been involved in a long-standing land dispute with the Jacksons, relatives of one of the Snowbird incumbents, Ned Long. Such disputes are unfortunate and painful for everyone involved. Thus, the potential existed for factionalizing the Snowbird community in the election.

I was again reminded of the upcoming election Monday night when about ten people gathered at the Snowbird Community Club to hear one of the candidates for vice chief, Leroy Wanetah. (Normally, 1973 would not have been a year for electing either a new principal chief or vice chief, since those are four-year-long offices, unlike the two-year-long council seats, but the position of vice chief had been vacated when the former principal chief, Noah Powell, died unexpectedly, and the then vice chief, John Crowe, had assumed the duties of chief.) Leroy Wanetah and his family apparently understood little of the Cherokee language since they spoke entirely in English. Snowbird Community Club meetings are usually conducted in the Cherokee language. The candidate began his speech by saying there should not be "hatred and jealousy" between Snowbird and the main reservation, the Qualla Boundary, implying that such sentiments might indeed exist. He dwelt on issues of little concern to Snowbird: the new Cherokee High School, which Snowbird children do not attend, and the tourist business, which focuses almost exclusively on the main reservation.

At one point Snowbird resident and then schoolteacher Gilliam Jackson asked the candidate why Indian children in Graham County had to pay a textbook fee in the Graham County Public Schools when it was the policy of the Bureau of Indian Affairs to fund Snowbird children's education with federal tax dollars as on the main reservation. The candidate's only suggested solution was for Graham County Indian students to travel, on their own, the one-hundred-mile round-trip each day to BIA schools in order to avoid paying the textbook fee in Graham County.

I was initially surprised when Jackson pressed Wanetah very aggressively, since I had never before seen him or anyone else from Snowbird act so blatantly assertive at a public gathering. Such behavior did not at first seem in keeping with the values of the Harmony Ethic. Jackson questioned the candidate repeatedly on his plans for the Snowbird community should he be elected. The candidate never outlined any specific plans, merely asserting repeatedly that he would "always work with the people" on any projects. Sociologist Murray Wax, in describing traditional Indian behavior among the Western Cherokees of Oklahoma has suggested that traditionalists who will not act assertively for their own benefit as individuals have no qualms about doing so as a spokesman for group interests, a condition that may explain the behavior I observed.[9]

The rest of the club's business meeting was held almost entirely in the Cherokee language, which meant the candidate, his family, and I all had trouble understanding the conversation. The only time the meeting again switched to English was to discuss the topic of housing with the candidate.

On September 6, the election was finally held. I was uncertain what the results might be but had begun to be concerned with the possible effects of two newspaper articles. The first of the two articles in the Band's official newspaper, the *Cherokee One Feather,* appeared in the August 29 edition, and the second article appeared on September 5, the day before the election. Twice the newspaper incorrectly reported that Snowbird and Tomotla would have two councilmembers apiece. The August 29 edition listed Snowbird (Graham County) candidates separately from Tomotla (Cherokee County) candidates, as was done for each of the five townships on the Qualla Boundary.[10] The September 5 edition further emphasized the ambiguous situation when it stated on the front page: "In a break from tradition, tribal members who live in Cherokee County will elect two council members. In the past they have been considered part of the Snowbird Township." To compound the confusion the headline stated: "Tribe to Elect . . . 14 Councilmen."[11] It should be noted that the township was referred to as the Snowbird, not Cheoah, Township, emphasizing the confusion many Qualla Boundary residents feel about community and political organizations off the main reservation. Even the *Asheville Citizen*, the major newspaper for western North Carolina, on September 7, the day after the election, reported the voting results for Graham and Cherokee Counties separately, demonstrating there was still confusion after the election about whether Snowbird and Tomotla were one township or not.

It was not until a week after the election, on September 12, that the *Cherokee One Feather* reported: "In an election story in the Sept. 5 issue the One Feather erroneously announced that Cherokee County had been designated a separate district [township] and would elect their own councilmen. The resolution asking for Cherokee County recognition was first tabled by the Tribal Council then withdrawn for revision. An amendment to the tribe's state charter under which the EBCI operates would be necessary to establish an additional township. This question will be one of the first to be taken up by the October Annual Council." In the next paragraph of the September 12 front-page story, however, the confusion over whether Snowbird and Tomotla were one township or not was perpetuated: "In last Tuesday's voting Mose Wachacha and Ned Long were picked in Snowbird and Bailey Coleman and Albert Martin were the big vote getters in Cherokee County."[12] Nowhere were the votes from both communities and for all four candidates tabulated together. No one reading the tribal newspaper a week after the election, therefore, knew who the two Cheoah Township councilmembers might be, if in fact the two communities were considered part of the same political district. It was October before Snowbird realized the full extent the election results might have on the community's political autonomy.

A significant number of Snowbird people, mistakenly thinking their two incumbents were running unopposed in the election, thought their votes were not needed and did not show up at the polls. In fact, the various newspaper accounts encouraged them in their thinking. When the results from both communities were finally tabulated together, two Tomotla men had won. Tribal Council confirmed this course of action and decided to swear in the two Tomotla men as Cheoah councilmembers. This was the surprising news I learned on my return to Snowbird on October 7 (after two weeks' absence from the area due to pneumonia).

I learned from the two Snowbird councilmembers that neither wished personally to push the election controversy before council but thought that Snowbird as a community should press the issue. Ned Long predicted possible dire consequences should Tomotla maintain control of the Cheoah council seats: health care services, the Head Start school, tribal-sponsored employment opportunities, and new house-building programs might all be shifted from Graham to Cherokee County. There were definite economic advantages to representation in council.

On the night of October 8, about fifteen Snowbird residents, all active members of the community club, met in the rescue squad building to discuss the council controversy and work out a strategy. They decided that Tribal Council's course of action was unacceptable to them. They chose to present their case to council during its session the next day, October 9. During the meeting I was asked to get a telephone call through to Principal Chief John Crowe, who has an unpublished number, so that one of the residents in attendance could tell him about Snowbird's grievance and ask for his support. The principal chief has kinsmen in Snowbird, and one of the Snowbird councilmembers, Ned Long, as well as others had vigorously supported him for election as vice chief in 1971. The group, therefore, logically looked to him for support. He promised to attend in order to voice their concerns to Tribal Council.

On Tuesday, October 9, I woke up at five in the morning to drive with a Snowbird resident, Gilliam Jackson, to Cherokee for the council session. At the time Gilliam Jackson, Ed and Ella Jackson's son, taught fifth grade at Robbinsville Elementary School in Graham County, the first Indian to hold such a position, and he was the first Snowbird Cherokee to have graduated from college. He had hurriedly arranged for a substitute teacher the night before in order to attend the council session. Other Snowbird residents also made the fifty-mile journey to Cherokee that morning, and the Snowbird group was under the leadership of a former councilmember and *gadugi* captain, Mason Ledford, a traditionalist who feels more comfortable speaking in Cherokee than English. Most of those in the Snowbird group were related in some way to the two Snowbird councilmembers, but since practically everyone in the approximately 350-person Snowbird community is related to everyone else by at least cousin ties, these kin relationships may or may not have been significant. It is important to note that neither of the Snowbird councilmembers attended to defend themselves. Snowbird traditionalists do not easily act assertively on their own behalf.

Many in the group who traveled to Cherokee had to miss a day's work and a day's pay. I remembered how Ned Long had complained that Saturday council sessions, more convenient to the distant Snowbird community and to anyone who worked for an employer, were never held. Several of the councilmembers from the main reservation own their own tourist-related businesses and never lose pay by attending council. Weekday sessions also leave them free for the weekend rush of tourists. Anyone traveling fifty miles each way from Snowbird for a council session cannot easily and quickly return to work for part of the day after council's business is concluded. Weekday sessions are perceived by Snowbird people as being for the convenience of the main reservation.

Dawn overtook us as we neared Cherokee, and we decided to have breakfast before proceeding to council. We stopped at the Teepee, one of the large restaurants that caters to the summer tourist trade, and one of the few to remain open for business year-round. We ended up eating with the Cherokee postmaster. The postmaster, Bo Parris, a non-Indian married to a Cherokee woman, speaks some Cherokee and is a Baptist minister at a church in the Big Cove community. Big Cove, like Snowbird, has a large number of fullbloods and Cherokee-speakers and has been the subject of several pieces of anthropological research on traditionalist Cherokees. The postmaster had preached at a Snowbird church the night before, and it is through attending each other's churches that many ties between Snowbird and main reservation fullbloods are maintained.

After some friendly banter with the postmaster about anthropologists, Gilliam Jackson and I drove over to the council house on Highway 441. Various tourist enterprises (shops, motels, and restaurants), strung out along highways 19 and 441, cluster tightly at the intersection of the two thoroughfares and are joined by the Bureau of Indian Affairs complex (offices, personnel's housing, and school buildings) and the structures representing the government of the Eastern Band of Cherokee Indians (council house, business offices, police department, and newspaper office).

Council met in a chamber down the hall from the offices of principal chief and vice chief. The spacious room was filled with rows of folding chairs where spectators, petitioners, and advisers sit. The chamber was a blend of modern and Indian qualities. The twelve councilmembers, including the one serving as chairman; an interpreter; an English (language) clerk; and an Indian (Cherokee-language) clerk all sat in large, leather swivel chairs behind a U-shaped table placed on a slightly raised platform. At the time the Indian clerk was elderly Maggie Axe Wachacha from Snowbird, who transcribed the proceedings in the Cherokee syllabary. She is related by marriage to Snowbird councilmember Mose Wachacha. The room's furnishings, including the framed photographs of the chief, vice chief, executive adviser, chairman of Tribal Council, and past chiefs, all gave the appearance of a newly furnished city council chamber. But the exposed wooden beams and the seven hand-carved Cherokee clan masks suspended from the ceiling lent to the room a rustic quality which was intended to remind everyone that this was an Indian council house.

Shortly before nine o'clock the room slowly began to fill with spectators, many of whom were from either Graham or Cherokee County. Almost all those from Graham County appeared Indian, while nearly all those from Cherokee County appeared white. Before council began, some Tomotla residents discussed the council election and boasted that only one of the two Snowbird incumbents had gotten any votes in Cherokee County and that he had received only one. I knew that together the three Tomotla candidates had gotten about a dozen votes in Graham County, mostly, I suspected, from Albert Martin's Snowbird in-laws.

Shortly after nine, council convened with one of its first orders of business, the swearing in of Bailey Coleman as a Cheoah councilmember. (The other Tomotla man, Albert Martin, had been sworn in at a previous session.) Martin looks quite Indian, and it is he who is married to the Snowbird woman. Coleman appears white.

It was after the swearing in of the Tomotla councilmember that Snowbird resident Mason Ledford was recognized and allowed to present his motion that the two Cheoah council seats be returned to Snowbird. The motion, full of legal jargon, was drawn up by a white Graham County attorney and read before council by the English clerk.

With one white Indian councilmember calling Snowbird a "bad sport" because the community would not admit that Tomotla had won a fair election, council nearly voted down the motion immediately. Even the newly elected vice chief, Leroy Wanetah, the same man I had heard address the Snowbird Community Club, termed Snowbird a "bad sport" before everyone present. Only a statement by Principal Chief John Crowe, prompted by the telephone conversation the night before, that

Snowbird might be considering a civil liberties lawsuit if the motion were defeated, encouraged council to delay its decision and call for the presentation of arguments from the Snowbird and Tomotla groups. Many of the councilmembers in attendance had little knowledge of the controversy, one even confessing he had not previously known of the existence of Indians in Cherokee County (demonstrating the previous lack of Indian identity there). With one coffee break and another break for lunch, the discussion over the council controversy lasted that day until about one-thirty in the afternoon. Although the principal chief had seen to it that Snowbird's case was heard, by means of the lawsuit threat, he nevertheless attempted to maintain a neutral pose by speaking of the need for council to deal fairly with both communities and to find a means for each to be satisfactorily represented in council.

The topic of immediate interest to everyone present was the past history of ties between Graham and Cherokee County Indians. After some time the tribal attorney and people from the two communities agreed on a history of the two groups' past voting practices: before 1951 those Tomotla people who were originally from the Qualla Boundary often went back to their Boundary townships, mostly Birdtown, to vote, which is about a sixty-mile trip each way. In 1951 Tomotla people in Cherokee County were allowed to journey the thirty miles to the next county, Graham, and the Snowbird community, and vote with the Cheoah Township for the two Cheoah council seats. This practice continued until 1971 when two separate polling places were established, one at Snowbird and one at Tomotla. That same year, 1971, Tomotla first attempted to run candidates for the Cheoah council seats, and at that time the rules of the 1897 amendment to the 1889 Cherokee Charter were successfully invoked by Snowbird to prevent Tomotla people from running since the amendment makes no reference to representation in tribal government for Tomotla. In 1973 Tomotla succeeded in running three candidates for the two Cheoah seats, and two of those candidates, Albert Martin and Bailey Coleman, the ones sponsored by the Tomotla Community Club, defeated the two Snowbird incumbents, Ned Long and Mose Wachacha.

After a rough history of the two groups' past voting practices had been pieced together, each group began to present its case. Each group sought the most advantageous legal argument it could present. Tomotla's argument that they could represent the Cheoah Township was based on the voting practices of the past twenty-two years which had Tomotla and

Snowbird voting for the same council seats. Snowbird's argument that only they could legally hold the Cheoah council seats was based on the seventy-six-year-old amendment to the 1889 Cherokee Charter. Tomotla, therefore, argued that the practices of the past twenty-two years had made it de facto part of the Cheoah settlement. Snowbird argued that the two communities were separate and distinct and that only Snowbird constituted the Cheoah settlement of Graham County mentioned in the charter's amendment. Snowbird thus argued from the position of a specific legal document while Tomotla argued from a position of common practice.

The style in which each group presented its arguments varied greatly. Speakers for Tomotla appeared openly antagonistic, chiding Snowbird for its poor representation of Tomotla in the past. Remarks were aggressive, as when the two Tomotla councilmembers said nothing Snowbird could do would ever make them give up their seats. At one point, one of the Tomotla councilmembers, Bailey Coleman, was asked if he thought Tomotla could represent the interests of both Tomotla and Snowbird. He joked that they would do for Snowbird all Snowbird had done for them in the past, implying Snowbird had not done much and now Tomotla might enjoy slighting Snowbird in the same manner. Snowbird's presented position was that although Snowbird deserved these two council seats, two more should be created for Tomotla since neither community was capable of representing the other properly. This argument apparently grew out of Snowbird's belief that white Indians (Tomotla) and real Indians (Snowbird) are two entirely different types of people. In contrast to Tomotla's speakers, those from Snowbird did not appear agitated, their voices never rising in anger. This type of calm behavior is normal for traditionalist Cherokees. The Snowbird group, who looked more Indian than those from Tomotla, consistently addressed council in the Cherokee language though most Snowbird residents speak fluent English. It was an exercise in impression management, as if they were publicly displaying that they were the real Indians in the controversy. Even a Big Cove councilmember, Wilbur Sequoyah, who supported Snowbird's position, addressed council in Cherokee though he too speaks English. Gilliam Jackson first addressed council in Cherokee and then translated his own speech into English when he found interpreter Mark Reed's translation inadequate, since Snowbird Cherokees speak a different dialect of Cherokee (Atali) than those on the Qualla Boundary (Kituhwa).

As Snowbird and Tomotla argued their cases, councilmembers from other communities frequently made references to communities who were grouped together into one township. Such a case is the "Thirty-two Hundred Acre Tract" (the Thomas Tract) and Birdtown proper that, although viewing themselves as separate communities, are both found within the Birdtown Township. Another such case is the Soco and Big "Y" areas which also see themselves as separate communities though both exist within the Wolfetown Township. After some vacillation one of the Wolfetown councilmembers suggested Soco and Big "Y" should also have separate councilmembers, as Snowbird and Tomotla wished for themselves. One of the councilmembers from Birdtown argued, however, that the Thirty-two Hundred Acre Tract and Birdtown proper should remain one township and that people in Birdtown proper would not be upset if candidates from the Thirty-two Hundred Acre Tract won both Birdtown council seats (although this has never happened). This same councilmember and others argued that if Snowbird and Tomotla and all other communities wishing their own representatives were set up as separate townships, council would become too large to function well. (If Cheoah, Birdtown, and Wolfetown were all split, there could be as many as eighteen councilmembers instead of the present twelve.) Another major problem expressed by various councilmembers was that the newly proposed townships, like the old ones, would not be proportioned by population. This last point was to become important in the final outcome of the case over a year later.

After a lunch break, the mother-in-law of Albert Martin asked to address council. She is also a Snowbird resident and is unique in having kinship ties with both communities. Only 1.5 percent of Snowbird adults are from Tomotla, and just 2.3 percent of the parents of Snowbird adults are from Tomotla. (In contrast, 12 percent of Snowbird adults are from the Qualla Boundary.) Like the other Snowbird residents, Martin's mother-in-law addressed council in the Cherokee language. She suggested that those Snowbird residents present at council were there only because they were the relatives of the two displaced Snowbird councilmembers and were not representative of the Snowbird community. She failed to mention, however, her own relationship with one of the Tomotla councilmembers. None of the others present from Snowbird pointed out publicly that she was a kinsman of one of the Tomotla councilmembers and therefore had a unique interest in how the controversy was solved. Instead, during a brief break, one of the Snowbird men explained the situation to one of the main reservation councilmembers.

Council could have voted on October 9 whether or not to accept Snowbird's petition for the return of its council seats. Instead, it tabled the matter for further consideration. Many of the councilmembers present expressed their concern over Snowbird's threat to take the case out of the hands of Tribal Council and into the hands of the federal courts. It therefore seemed unwise to rule against Snowbird. Tomotla, however, made it seem equally unwise to rule against the Cherokee County group by also threatening a lawsuit. Council was unsure which side to support and which to alienate.

At that point the local superintendent for the Bureau of Indian Affairs reminded council that the Eastern Band had never written and adopted a new constitution under the requirements of the 1934 Indian Reorganization Act (Wheeler-Howard Act) although it had voted to do so; there was a possibility that the whole voting and districting structure of the reservation was thus illegal and that such an illegality would be exposed if the whole controversy went to federal court. (Tribal Council sometimes seems to enjoy the fact it has never formally reorganized under the Wheeler-Howard Act, since not doing so makes the Eastern Band's status ambiguous and may actually allow the Band to exert its authority in gray areas which exist because the Band has not reorganized.) This fact would assist either side in suing. Faced with no obvious choice it could make in its own best interest, Tribal Council delayed a decision and tabled the matter.

THE ANALYSIS

During much of the council session I found myself getting quite agitated, especially over the way the Snowbird representatives presented their case, since my own inclination would have been to voice Snowbird's views more assertively. When simultaneously confronted with the values of the Harmony Ethic and the need to act atypically assertively, Snowbird chose to act assertively, but reluctantly. People who would not have acted even that assertively in their own interests as individuals were nevertheless willing to do so for the good of the group, the entire Snowbird community.

After the council session of October 9, 1973, I occasionally heard news of more developments in the council controversy. On the evening of November 5, I attended a Snowbird Community Club meeting and was surprised to find some Cherokee County Indians in attendance, something I had never before witnessed. One of the Tomotla councilmembers, Albert Martin, was present, the one with in-laws in Graham County, and was seated between his parents-in-law. Atypically, the club meeting was conducted in English rather than Cherokee. The main topic of the meeting was the Qualla Housing Authority which had recently announced it could not build any more houses until delinquent payments were made on houses already built. Some Cherokee County people, who had not previously had access to the housing program, probably as a result of not being directly represented in council, here accused Snowbird residents of not paying on time and ruining the future of low-cost housing. At that point the Snowbird community BIA representative, a non-Indian, pointed out that a smaller percentage (and smaller number) of Snowbird people were behind on payments than were residents of the main reservation, the Qualla Boundary.

After a lull in building housing, which lasted for more than a year after that community club meeting, the housing authority did arrange for 175 more family units to be constructed, and the January 29, 1975, edition of the *Cherokee One Feather* announced that some of the units would be placed in Cherokee County.[13] By the end of 1975 new houses were under construction in the Tomotla community. Before more active participation in tribal affairs, through council representation, Tomotla had been largely ignored by the housing authority, which is located on the main reservation. In addition, the May 5, 1976, edition of the *Cherokee One Feather* announced that a $73,600 grant from the federal government to the Eastern Band would be used to construct a new community center in Cherokee County.[14] The construction of the center and high quality family housing for Tomotla seems to be the direct result of representation on Tribal Council, and Tomotla continues to benefit economically from its involvement in tribal government.

Prior to 1975, the Qualla Housing Authority, formed in 1962, had been responsible for helping build or significantly improve over four hundred houses. Thus, in the time period from the formation of the authority until 1975, the fraction of substandard housing on the Eastern Cherokee reservation was reduced from nearly 90 to less than 60 percent.[15] The additional 175 family houses, plus 25 more units for the elderly, proposed for 1975, reduced even further the percentage of sub-standard housing.[16] By 1990 the Qualla Housing Authority had built more than 1,100 houses throughout the reservation, and the building continues.

The Qualla Housing Authority is, therefore, a rather large-scale, long-term operation in which Cherokee County residents logically wanted to be included. Access to the Authority and the subsequent building of new houses has to be rated as one of the major economic incentives motivating people in the 1973 political controversy. Since 1973 many Tomotla people have met the requirements and applied for housing.

To qualify for a new house under the program, at least one member of a household must be an enrolled Eastern Cherokee (the minimal Indian blood degree for which is one-sixteenth) and have possessory rights to a tract of reservation land upon which the house can be built. In addition, a family must put many hours of labor into the building of the semi-prefabricated home. Tribal-sponsored low-cost loans are also available. Before active participation in council, many in Cherokee County may not have even been familiar with the requirements for new housing. Most of the houses, ranging from two to four bedrooms, include a living-dining area, kitchen, bathroom, and carport and have electricity, central heating, hot water, and indoor plumbing. By 1976 many were built of bricks, and in the 1980s a few two-story homes were built. In other words, access to the housing program would afford many families who identified as Cherokee Indians an opportunity to improve significantly their standard of living, a chance which for many would not be available from other more expensive sources. By 1975, nearly 29 percent of all occupied houses in Snowbird had been built through the Qualla Housing Authority (according to figures derived from an unpublished housing survey conducted by the Eastern Band of Cherokee Indians in 1974). Tomotla wanted a similar situation in Cherokee County. It is interesting that although the figure for substandard housing for the Eastern Band as a whole at the time approached 60 percent, substandard housing for Snowbird was less than 43 percent, a statistic which reinforces the image of Snowbird as a successful, adaptive community.

Low cost, good quality housing is not the only benefit derived from Band membership and political representation on Tribal Council. One of the more tangible economic advantages was the Indian Claims Commission money awarded to the Eastern Band (over $1,800,000). The Eastern

Cherokees voted in 1972 (only a year before the election involving the council controversy) to accept the amount offered by the federal government, and shortly thereafter Tribal Council voted for a per capita distribution of the money to Band members. Each per capita share came to about $200. Only two councilmembers, Mose Wachacha and Ned Long from Snowbird, both traditionalists, voted that the money be used for some communal goal, such as purchasing more reservation land. Other suggestions made by traditionalists demonstrated their ability to subscribe to the values of the Harmony Ethic, such as putting the group ahead of the individual, while simultaneously acting adaptively within the framework of modern American society. Traditionalists correctly assumed that a per capita distribution would spread the money too thinly and soon it would be gone. Instead they suggested the money be invested corporately, and the interest earned be used for college scholarships and to supplement the elderly's social security payments. White Indians were not interested in these proposals by traditionalists. It should be noted that shortly after such per capita distributions of money to the Eastern Cherokees and other Native American groups, strictly per capita distributions were opposed by Indian activists like Vine Deloria, Jr., and ultimately outlawed for other groups by the federal government.

By early 1974 (shortly after the two Cherokee County men were seated as the Cheoah councilmembers) tribal government intensified efforts to enroll people in anticipation of the per capita allotment of the Indian Claims Commission money: "before the money can be distributed here, the roll [the Baker Roll of the 1920s] must be brought current as of the date the plan is approved by the Congress."[17] The Baker Roll itself was challenged in the 1920s and 1930s by many fullbloods who claimed that some individuals enrolled as Eastern Cherokees did not have the minimum, or any, Cherokee blood degree.

In the August 14, 1974, issue, the *Cherokee One Feather* reported on a vote taken in Tribal Council on a resolution that "no one who is less than one-sixteenth Cherokee blood share in claims money."[18] One-sixteenth provable Cherokee blood degree is the minimum for an individual to be enrolled as a member of the Eastern Band of Cherokee Indians. The resolution was killed with only one councilmember voting for the resolution. The results of the vote obviously favor not only white Indians, but whites of Indian descent, not fullbloods or a fullblood community like Snowbird, which at that time had no representation of its own on

Tribal Council. The results of the vote, in effect, encouraged distribution of claims money to individuals who were not members of the Eastern Band, whose ancestors married outside of the Band too frequently and disinherited their descendents from legally being Cherokee Indians.

From November 1973 until early January 1974 during my fieldwork residence, I heard little about the council controversy. On the night of January 10, however, I was invited to attend an informal meeting of four Snowbird residents at the community club building to discuss council's recent decision formally killing Snowbird's resolution for reinstatement of its councilmembers. Of the four men present, one was one of the displaced councilmembers, Ned Long; another was a former *gadugi* captain who had previously served in council, Mason Ledford (the same who had led the Snowbird group in presenting the resolution to council); another was a Snowbird community health representative, William Jackson, hired by the Band; and the fourth was active in various community affairs. They ranged in age from their twenties to their fifties. (The youngest, William Jackson, another of Ed and Ella Jackson's sons, had invited me to attend.) The discussion was mostly in Cherokee with shifts to English to explain to me Snowbird's resolution and the recent statement of the Bureau of Indian Affairs attorney that argued against Snowbird's position.

Council, concerned about the Band's chances in federal court against one of its own communities, had consulted Bureau of Indian Affairs lawyers for their opinions on Snowbird's chances of winning a lawsuit. When the attorneys assessed Snowbird's chances as nil, council voted down Snowbird's resolution and recognized the two men from Tomotla as the legal Cheoah councilmembers. The four Snowbird men who met informally that evening did so to consider Snowbird's next strategic move. In the spirit of the Harmony Ethic, the group decided to give council one last chance to reconsider its position before going to court. The group realized that a court case, even if won, might antagonize the Qualla Boundary Cherokees and jeopardize any current or future benefits Snowbird might derive from the Eastern Band. (I was asked, if necessary, to present research to show that historically Snowbird and Tomotla are separate communities, but although I shared my idea, that the Snowbird Mountains served as the southern boundary for pre-removal traditionalist Cherokees, with one of the men, I was never asked to prepare a formal statement.)

Nothing further was done by the Snowbird community to solve the council controversy until after I completed my fieldwork in late February 1974. On the morning of February 4, however, when I was in Cherokee, a linguist friend William Cook and I encountered Lloyd Owle, a prominent Qualla Boundary leader, local director of the Save the Children Fund, and an eloquent spokesperson for the white Indian position. Over coffee at the Teepee Restaurant, the conversation turned to the council controversy. Owle is a minimal-blood-degree Cherokee with blonde hair and fair skin who does not speak the Cherokee language but is obviously proud of his Cherokee heritage. He also works hard for the benefit of all Cherokee children, including those in Snowbird. A native of Birdtown, he told me one of his great-grandfathers was from the Tomotla area of Cherokee County. When the topic of the council controversy arose, he openly sided with Cherokee County's position, seeing the entire controversy as yet another example of fullbloods versus white Indians like himself. He viewed the case as another attempt by fullbloods to gain power and positions from white Indians just because fullbloods were fullbloods. (Fullbloods similarly say they are the only real Indians.) Owle asserted that if the white Indians ever banded together into a political coalition the way the fullbloods do, the white Indians could easily run everything since they outnumber fullbloods.

When I reminded Owle that Snowbird might choose to sue the Band over the council controversy, he brushed aside the suggestion that the community might actually succeed in circumventing council's decision. He also suggested, accurately, that Snowbird's position might even worsen if the community won a lawsuit. Revising the charter to provide Snowbird and Tomotla each with two councilmembers, he argued, would leave the way clear for other revisions in the charter, many of which could harm Snowbird and other fullblood groups. The major revision that would come about, he suggested, would be the reduction in blood-degree requirements for principal chief and vice chief from one-half blood degree to one-fourth or less, on grounds that the present policy was discriminatory against some Band members like himself. Such a revision, he argued, would hurt fullbloods more than any benefits they might gain from maintaining two fullblood council seats. These were just the types of retaliatory ideas that some people in Snowbird feared would result from a court case. In fact, since then the one-half blood-degree requirement for chief and vice chief has been dropped, and any enrolled Band member may run for the offices. In 1987 Jonathan Ed Taylor, during the 1973 controversy a councilmember from Wolfetown, became the first Eastern Cherokee Chief of less than one-half blood degree.

Owle also referred to the same problem of redistricting I had previously heard voiced in council. If Cheoah were split into two communities with two representatives in council apiece, then Wolfetown would want to split into two new townships, as would Birdtown.

When I mentioned the ambiguous newspaper articles which had presented a misleading view of the council election, I was assured by him that no one had really been confused by them.

Next, I asked Owle his opinions of Snowbird people in general, apart from the council controversy, and he gave a description repeated by many people. First, he distinguished them from fullbloods in another major fullblood community, Big Cove. Even many Snowbird fullbloods make this distinction. Others have described non-Snowbird fullbloods stereotypically as crazy, mean, and dangerous, people to be avoided because of their supposedly high incidence of "abnormal" traits like alcoholism, violence, homicide, and suicide.[19] The Cherokee leader described Snowbird people, in contrast, as hard-working and Snowbird as a "good place to live." He said, as do many others, that Snowbird people even speak a "purer" form of Cherokee than main reservation Indians.[20] He asserted that Snowbird is most successful in standing on its own and dealing with local whites, and that since the community can take care of itself, the main reservation is almost reluctant to assist Snowbird. He said that many on the Qualla Boundary are actually jealous of Snowbird and ask why the Band should help Snowbird out when the community is already so successful in helping itself. (The use of the word "jealous" is interesting since Leroy Wanetah, the candidate for vice chief, from the main reservation, who spoke at Snowbird also referred to hatred and jealousy between the main reservation and Snowbird.)

Owle is not unfamiliar with Snowbird or its people. His job in aiding Cherokee children and working with community development clubs like Snowbird's frequently takes him to the community and to many other areas of the reservation. Many Snowbird children derive greatly needed financial benefits from the Save the Children money distributed by Owle, and his concern for those children and the Eastern Band cannot be doubted.

My formal fieldwork came to a close in late February 1974, but although I am not living on the Cherokee reservation, I have kept in contact with many people there through short visits, letters, telephone conversations, and the *Cherokee One Feather*. During such a telephone conversation in February of 1975, I discovered that Snowbird had taken its case to federal court, at Bryson City in Swain County, and appeared to have won its case, although it was under appeal by the Band.

Later, in April of 1975, I received another telephone call, from the Longs, and news of the controversy was more gloomy for Snowbird. A judge in Bryson City ruled that the two Tomotla men had been elected fairly to the positions of Cheoah councilmembers. Apparently the fact that Snowbird appeared to outnumber Tomotla in eligible voters convinced the judge that the Snowbird candidates had a fair chance of winning and that their losing the election simply demonstrated a lack of support for the Snowbird men. Besides the judge's ruling in favor of Tomotla, there was another important outcome of the case. The court ruled that because of disproportionate populations in each township, efforts to create a one-man, one-vote situation in tribal elections would have to be made through redistricting the townships, or some other plan. By August of 1975, I learned that a still higher court had ruled in favor of Snowbird, that under the Cherokee Charter Tomotla was not part of the Cheoah Township. So Snowbird won its case, but only one month before the 1975 elections. The judge also ruled, however, that Tomotla could not continue to be disfranchised and upheld the other court's ruling that a one-man, one-vote situation be created in tribal elections.

Tribal Council decided to keep the six traditional townships with twelve councilmembers rather than redistrict the population. Instead, to create equal representation, the vote of a councilmember representing fewer people now counts less than that of someone representing more people. In this situation councilmembers from a smaller township, like Cheoah (including now officially both Snowbird and Tomotla), have a vote in council which will count only three-fourths of a point while someone from one of the larger townships might have a vote worth one or one and a half points. The biennial elections for Tribal Council were held again in September of 1975, and Snowbird people were planning strategies six months in advance. Two of the younger men active in the council controversy were considering running, but both said that in any case Snowbird should run only two candidates so as not to divide the community's vote and allow Tomotla to win the seats again. One of these men, schoolteacher and Cherokee traditionalist, Gilliam Jackson, did run as one of the two Snowbird candidates and was elected. A Tomotla man, the incumbent white Indian Bailey Coleman, took the other council seat. The result of the 1975 election, a winner from each of the two communities, was reminiscent of Tomotla's original offer to Snowbird to split the two Cheoah seats. Since 1975 every council election has seen one Cheoah councilmember from Snowbird and one from Tomotla. It should also be pointed out that many in Snowbird say the various Tomotla councilmembers over the years have treated Snowbird fairly.

Under pressure from the courts, the Eastern Band legally combined Tomotla and Snowbird into the Cheoah Township, and Snowbird's alternative suggestions for including Tomotla in Band affairs were not considered. This consequence plus the point system which reduced the worth of the Cheoah councilmembers' votes might appear to mean Snowbird ended up in a worse position in having chosen to turn to the courts. Clearly Snowbird now has less political power on Tribal Council with only three-fourths of a vote rather than two votes. Given the information with which Snowbird was working at the time, however, the community probably made a rational choice, realizing that any choice they made in that situation involved a risk.

In 1971 Snowbird had been successful in preventing a Tomotla man from running for a Cheoah council seat simply by invoking the 1897 amendment to the 1889 Cherokee Charter. Since that type of argument had proven successful in 1971, it was logical to use it again in 1973 in almost identical circumstances. The fact that, technically, the community won its case, if only a Pyrrhic victory, indicates the choice was a rational one. The major risk anticipated in resorting to the courts was the possibility of economic reprisals by the rest of the Band. Snowbird simply did not have enough data to anticipate fully the risk of the point system for council voting. (Perhaps no individual ever makes a truly rational decision since no one can ever be certain of having all the information affecting any choice.)

The controversy has demonstrated that traditionalist fullblood communities can act assertively, rationally weigh the constraints and incentives at work on any decision, and finally choose a strategic, adaptive course of action. This is in contrast to the image often presented of traditionalist Cherokees. Snowbird people are not passive conservative Indians who, when frustrated in important undertakings turn to alcohol and misdirected violence.[21] Instead, the community channels its efforts positively. Such actions do not mean the Snowbird Cherokees will always win, but it means they have a chance of accomplishing their goals. It is also important to remember that this assertive behavior comes about despite a desire to be harmony-oriented and non-aggressive. The major choice Snowbird made was whether or not the situation was important enough to the whole group to act assertively, a condition of the Harmony Ethic.

The 1975 council election results were interesting in that one Snowbird man, a fullblood, and one Tomotla man, an incumbent white Indian elected in 1973, each won one of the two Cheoah seats. Two other men also ran for the seats, one from Snowbird and one from Tomotla, the other incumbent. Although I did not witness the 1975 election as I did the 1973 one, I surmise that in the 1975 election, issues other than those specifically relating to the two communities' rivalry dominated. Apparently, many people in both communities have realized that continuing to jockey for complete control of the council seats for their own communities would simply channel everyone's energies into a possible losing battle every two years. Many people assumed the best way to win in 1975 would be to run two individuals, one from each community, as a unit. If such strategies remain the normal course of action, as they have for the last fifteen years, Snowbird will at least maintain one council seat without much difficulty and without the real Indian–white Indian factionalism which rips apart the Big Cove community every two years. Part of the Snowbird community's current strategy involves a kind of pragmatism and a continued emphasis on harmony.

The particular situation of the council session at which Snowbird presented its petition to restore its council seats (as well as the events that preceded and followed that occasion) illustrates most of what is crucial concerning intraethnic relations on the Eastern Cherokee reservation and one traditionalist Cherokee community's views of its own identity. That event represents a microcosm of intercommunity and intraethnic boundary maintenance among the Eastern Cherokee Indians.

If there is one significant quality that characterizes an individual Eastern Cherokee's relations with nearly everyone he meets, it is probably a tendency to type each person somewhere along a red-white continuum.

Sometimes this tendency is also applied to whole communities or groups of people. The only two significant ethnic groups in southwestern North Carolina are Native American Cherokees and white Appalachians.

From the Cherokees' point of view, however, there are many people who are not easily classified as white or Indian. This tendency to view some people as not quite white or Indian is applied to minimal-blood-degree members of the Eastern Band of Cherokee Indians. In fact, some fullbloods refer only to themselves as Indians and refuse to apply the term to individuals of minimal blood degree. Sociologist Laurence French estimates the conservative fullblood population as making up one-third of the total Cherokee population (about three thousand people) and assumes that those white Indians who have also achieved truly middle-class status are even less numerous than the conservative full-bloods.[22] If "real Indianness" is judged by another important scale besides blood degree, namely ability to speak the Cherokee language, linguist Duane King estimates only one-ninth of the total Cherokee popula-tion (less than one thousand people) are real Indians by virtue of being Cherokee-language speakers. Other qualities of "real Indianness" are even harder to figure statistically. How many people are classified as real Indians, for example, because they "act Indian"?

This tendency among Cherokees to type people, apparent in the politi-cal controversy just described, reflects the factions within the Eastern Band. Disparate political, economic, and social conditions often existing between the two extreme factions of fullbloods and white Indians create disagreements and distrust and sometimes develop into open contro-versies. The particular controversy described here probably developed when the prospect of great economic advantages, like access to new housing or Claims Commission money, urged a white Indian commu-nity to attempt to seize political power from a fullblood community. The prospect of losing political power within the Eastern Band and the resulting economic advantages of such power prompted the fullblood community to resist the attempts of the white Indian community. The conflict illustrates many of the reasons for the polarization of minimal-blood-degree and maximal-blood-degree people throughout the Chero-kee reservation.

Until the recent controversy, the Snowbird community, as a group of people predominantly fullblood, had a major advantage over other full-blood communities: Snowbird existed as a geographically, legally, and politically distinct unit within the Eastern Band as the Cheoah Township. Other Cherokee fullblood communities exist within political boundaries that also enclose significant numbers of white Indians. Until recently the Cheoah Township consistently sent two fullblood councilmembers to Tribal Council. As a result, all Cherokee fullbloods, whether from Snowbird or not, could be absolutely sure of having at least two people on council to voice the concerns of fullbloods. Within other townships, political factions divided along blood-degree lines continually jockey for control of council seats. Gulick has described the "Qualla Group," a faction of fullbloods who attempt to win political offices for fullbloods.[23] An analogy can be made between the functions of the Qualla Group and the instance described above when a fullblood councilmember from Big Cove sided with Snowbird in its dispute while his white Indian councilmate from Big Cove took a stand against Snowbird. Many of the impromptu political meetings which preceded the September 1973 election apparently involved fullblood groups who discussed means of maintaining or improving their position in council. The election of fullblood councilmember Wilbur Sequoyah from Big Cove may have been the result of efforts of these groups. Until recently the exact correspondence of the Snowbird community with the Cheoah Township meant the almost automatic election of fullbloods to two of the twelve council seats. Snowbird's loss of control, therefore, meant a loss of political power not only for one fullblood community but for fullbloods in general.

These circumstances may in part explain why the two Snowbird councilmembers were unwilling to compromise with Tomotla and have each community take one of the two seats, a situation that has since resulted. Such a compromise was probably not in the best interest of the Snowbird community at the time. Such a decision would have meant the permanent disappearance of Snowbird as a political entity by recognizing Tomotla's right to power; the potential persistent loss of power in the future; and the promise of political bickering of the type existing in other townships with blood-degree factionalism. The fact that no one from the Snowbird community suggested this type of obvious compromise to council demonstrates how unpalatable the alternative appeared. Such a decision was not in the community's best interest. The compromise Snowbird persistently suggested was that Tomotla be organized as a township and given its own two councilmembers while Snowbird maintained the two Cheoah council seats. Since there are a few maximal-blood-degree Cherokees in Tomotla, white Indians would not always be guaranteed control of those seats while two fullbloods from Snowbird would once again be certain to occupy seats in council. (In fact, only one of the two Tomotla men who were elected to the Cheoah council seats appears white, while the other, who looks like an Indian, has in-laws from Snowbird.) Whether or not Tomotla was given two new council seats, however, it was imperative for Snowbird to attempt to maintain control of two council seats of its own.

The main reservation, the Qualla Boundary, where minimal-blood-degree Cherokees form a much larger percentage of the population than in Snowbird, was reluctant to create two new council seats for the Band's outlying communities. This is probably true for at least two reasons. First, for white Indians on the Boundary, the new situation in which white Indians in the outlying areas have a chance of controlling the formerly fullblood monopoly on two council seats must have seemed an improved situation. Second, the Qualla Boundary probably viewed both Snowbird and Tomotla almost as types of off-reservation groups who should not have too great a share of the power in tribal affairs, since many of the concerns of the main reservation, such as tourism, are not concerns of Snowbird or Tomotla. The example of the main reservation councilmember who had not even known of the existence of Tomotla demonstrates how many main-reservation people do not distinguish clearly between the two communities, merely viewing them as one non-Boundary group. Since Snowbird and Tomotla together probably constitute less than one-twentieth of the Band's enrolled members, the Qualla Boundary probably viewed a decision which would have given the two communities together two-sevenths of the seats in the council (four seats out of fourteen) as unjustifiable. It was to the main reservation's and its white Indian population's advantage not to have created two new council seats for Tomotla and not to have restored the old ones to Snowbird's exclusive control.

The Tomotla community's success in capturing the two Cheoah council seats is evidence of the community's growing concern for enhancing its political and economic best interests. The economic advantages which lured Tomotla are largely similar to the ones Snowbird possessed: a Head Start school providing employment for several community residents and education and day care for community children, various tribal-sponsored employment opportunities, a local health care program, and especially access to Indian Claims Commission money, and access to the tribal-sponsored, low-cost housing program. The control of political power within tribal government on the part of Tomotla would help in-sure that these and other economic programs did not continue to bypass the Cherokee County community. As has been observed, some Snow-bird residents feared that Tomotla's dominance of the Cheoah Township council seats would mean simply shifting Snowbird's programs over to Tomotla, something in Tomotla's best interests but not Snowbird's. After all, in the case of housing opportunities, it has only been since Tomotla's rise to political power that new houses were first built in the community in 1975.

Although Snowbird urged a political compromise that would have given each of the two communities adequate power to pressure for eco-nomic advantages, Tomotla has chosen to work out a different solution, one more in its own best interests. Under the present 1889 Cherokee Charter and the 1897 amendment, the Cherokee County community probably does not have an adequate population of enrolled members of the Eastern Band to justify the organization of a seventh township. At the time the United States Census showed seventy-one Indians residing in Cherokee County, while tribal rules require a minimum population of a hundred.[24] (Interestingly, the 1980 United States Census shows an Indian population of 189.) Snowbird had sufficient numbers to go it alone with over 320 people. Tomotla probably thought it could not have a political voice in council (due to insufficient population) without being attached to Snowbird. The dominance of the Cheoah council seats at Snowbird's expense was Tomotla's only realistic choice during the 1973 elections.

Each political unit (the main reservation townships and the two Cheoah Township communities) and each ethnic faction (fullbloods and white Indians) attempted to accomplish what seemed in its own best interests the day that the council controversy was argued before Tribal Council. Each chose arguments that enhanced and justified its position, and the style in which each group presented its case reflected many of the dif-ferences in attitudes and goals that divide these groups in this and other matters of tribal importance.

Snowbird's logical choice for a legal argument before council was based on the 1897 amendment to the 1889 Cherokee Charter in which no mention of Cherokee County or the Tomotla community is made.[25] It is a legal argument by means of which the community hoped to regain its council seats, and an approach that had proven successful in 1971. The argument was thus an expression of the community's position within the realm of American law and did not fully reflect all the reasons for which Snowbird engaged in the controversy. Although Snowbird's legal argument necessarily revolved around community and county boundaries, what was at stake were ethnic boundaries separating real Indians and white Indians.

Tomotla's only realistic argument before council was based on the practices of the past two decades that represent a kind of newly evolving informal tradition conflicting with the formal Cherokee Charter and its amendment. The Cherokee County community's case was based on the voting habits of the past two decades during which Tomotla and Snowbird had been voting for the same council seats. Before Snowbird and Tomotla began voting together, Tomotla was completely unrepresented in Tribal Council and could not even vote for principal chief and vice chief. Tomotla logically argued that if people from both communities vote for the same representatives, then people from either community should be able to run and be elected as a representative.

The majority of Tribal Council, which later voted to quash Snowbird's proposal to return its council seats, also presented rational arguments for its point of view. The main opposition that these councilmembers cited for their action was the unfortunate precedent which would be set if Snowbird won its case. Should such happen, something would have to be done for the disfranchised Tomotla group, such as Snowbird's suggestion that a new township be created. If this were done for Tomotla, similar actions could be justified for at least two other townships, creating nine townships with eighteen representatives where once there were six townships with twelve representatives. This would reduce the influence of any one councilmember. Should the Cherokee Charter and its amendment that from every community of one hundred people two councilmembers be elected be taken literally, then conceivably, with an enrolled population at the time of about eight thousand, eighty townships with 160 councilmembers could be created. When the Cherokee population numbered only about a thousand people, six townships with twelve representatives came closer to approximating this provision.[26] When Bureau of Indian Affairs attorneys assessed Snowbird's chances of winning a court battle as minimal, these councilmembers voted down Snowbird's proposal.

Throughout the Eastern Cherokee area, Cherokees themselves largely speak of two groups whom they term fullbloods (sometimes real Indians or simply Indians) and white Indians (occasionally derogatively termed "five-dollar Indians"). Fullbloods are called that by themselves and by white Indians, and the term white Indians is applied both by that group and by fullbloods. There are a few individuals whom their fellow Cherokees find difficult to classify, but usually everyone can be classified. These groupings are largely by supposed blood degree. The ability or inability to speak the Cherokee language is, however, nearly as important. Behavior and values are also considered. There are realistic reasons for the fullblood–white Indian dichotomy.

A close look at the Tomotla community's recent history of relations with the Eastern Band of Cherokee Indians, as contrasted with Snowbird's, gives some clues. Tomotla, a predominantly white Indian group, has not always been so eager to establish ties with the Eastern Band. Legally the residents of Tomotla are Indians; physically they mostly look white. This duality of identity gives most Tomotla people, like other white Indians, an option not available to fullbloods; they can choose whether to be Indian or white. This phenomenon has little to do with behavioral types and much to do with economics. Tomotla is in a position to ask itself, is there more advantage to being Indian or white? Depending on the times and situation, either identity can be more to its advantage. At present, there is a continuing continent-wide movement for the improvement of Native American status and self-image. And, locally, there are many economic advantages to being Indian: tribal-supported employment, and health, educational, and housing opportunities. The Tomotla community has found a way to tap these opportunities by asserting its Indian identity and seeking and acquiring power within tribal government. At least in the case of housing this choice had, only one year later, already proved beneficial. Only two years later it had proved beneficial in the form of a new community center and, of course, the per capita distribution of Indian Claims Commission funds.

In the past it was often better to identify as white, and the census records' fluctuations in Cherokee County Indian population may represent the community's fluctuations in ethnic identity. Fullbloods' references to white Indians, like those in Tomotla, as "five-dollar Indians" reflects the perception of white Indians as people who, at least symbolically, can buy their way into the Indian community when the occasion requires or sell out to the white world if there is more advantage in that. Even as early as the Swetland Roll of 1869, and probably much earlier, most Indians in Cherokee County were minimal-blood-degree Cherokees. In 1950 the United States Census Bureau numbered only twenty-four Indians in the Tomotla community, and not for the previous half century had the community numbered more than sixty people classified as Indians. But in 1960 the community appeared to have more than doubled in size to sixty-two Indians. (Granted, the jump from the figures in 1950 to those in 1960 may have been due in part to self-identification of ethnic group on the census, which was first instituted in 1960.)

The jump from 1970 to 1980, however, the years that encompass Tomotla's search for political power, is even more dramatic, from 71 in 1970 to 189 in 1980, a 166.2 percent increase. In 1973 Tomotla was able to muster enough people to the polls to defeat the neighboring fullblood Snowbird community of 320 people. Before the election some Snowbird people were estimating Tomotla's population at around 500. No one was clear if the census count of 71 or Snowbird's estimate of 500 was more accurate. And it is still not clear to many in Snowbird how many people residing on reservation lands in Cherokee County are enrolled Eastern Cherokee Indians or merely white relatives or in-laws. For such a wide divergence in population estimates as 71 and 500, surely some Tomotla individuals must be vacillating in their identification as Indian or white. In other words, until recently, many people in the community were probably identifying as white, even to census-takers.

This situation may be true of white Indians in general and not just of the Tomotla community. Official United States Census Bureau records for 1970 showed 3,245 Indians residing in the four North Carolina counties where reservation lands are located. Official Band Enrollment Office records for about the same time period showed "over 7,000 enrolled members, with an estimated 5,000 living on or immediately adjacent to the Cherokee Indian lands."[27] The discrepancy between census and enrollment figures for just the local Cherokee population is over 1,700 people. This may mean that significant numbers of Cherokees are identifying as whites if the occasion permits and as Indians when the occasion demands, such as to the Band's Enrollment Office. Not to identify as Cherokee to the Band's Enrollment Office would be to sever important economic ties forever.

In a letter, Nampeo McKenney, Chief of the Racial Statistics Staff of the Bureau of the Census in 1975, explains: "The concept of race as used by the Bureau reflects self-identification. Since information on race was obtained by self-enumeration in the [1970] census, respondents had the opportunity to identify their own race. Persons who reported that they were American Indians were asked to give their tribe. . . . In those cases where the respondent failed to provide an entry on race, the information on race was obtained by the enumerator and, for the most part, by observation." Since self-enumeration has been the norm since the 1960 census, inaccuracies caused by census-takers should have been greatly reduced, despite some cases in which census-taker identification by observation is still used. Self-identification was urged by many Native Americans for quite some time, especially since other methods have tended to eliminate off-reservation Indians from a Native American classification.[28] New Census Bureau techniques should have decreased the discrepancy between official and tribal population counts more than it appears to have done. This seems, therefore, to be another reason to assume many "white Indians" are intentionally having themselves listed as white on census rolls, just as they occasionally present themselves as white when interacting with non-Indians other than census-takers.

In comparing the census figures for 1970 and 1980, Cherokee County is the most impressive with a 166.2 percent increase. Swain County's Indian population increased by 151.2 percent, and Jackson County's by 29.8 percent. The Snowbird population in Graham County increased the least, by only 18.4 percent. It is interesting to speculate that the dramatic increase in population, most noticeable in white Indian areas, was due not to a literal increase in population but to an increase in individuals willing to identify as Indian. The per capita distribution of Indian Claims Commission money to the Eastern Cherokees in the years between 1970 and 1980 may have been an incentive to many to identify more consistently as Indians.

The important thing, however, as Fredrik Barth has pointed out in similar cases, is not the real or imagined behavioral or cultural differences between two groups, like white Indians and real Indians: "The critical focus . . . becomes the ethnic *boundary* that defines the group, not the cultural stuff that it encloses."[29] With a group like Tomotla many individuals can choose to group themselves within the boundaries of the Eastern Cherokees or can withdraw and group themselves with the white community.

The manner in which the fullblood Snowbird group and the white Indian Tomotla group chose to present their cases in the council controversy demonstrates both the real and contrived differences between the two groups and how these differences were manipulated by each group to establish its boundaries. The manner in which Tomotla and Snowbird presented their cases to Tribal Council demonstrates how distinct are the boundaries that separate the two communities.

Yet why should Snowbird, as a fullblood community, try so persistently to separate itself from Tomotla, the white Indian community? Why do Eastern Cherokees perceive blood-degree factions as significant, and why do they exist throughout the reservation and historically for such a long period of time? Though rarely does an entire Cherokee community, such as Tomotla, choose between emphasizing or deemphasizing its Indian identity, some Cherokee individuals are continually confronted with the choice. Most of these individuals are the so-called white Indians, people with minimal Cherokee blood degree. They look white, speak English fluently (and rarely speak any Cherokee), and, most importantly, conform to white American cultural standards, i.e. they act white. These individuals can usually be accepted as white simply by ignoring their Cherokee background. Cherokees with maximal blood degree do not have this choice. Physically, they appear Indian, often speak Cherokee, or speak English with a Cherokee accent, and, most importantly, conform to Indian behavioral patterns, i.e. they act Indian. These fullbloods often resent white Indians who can alternate between two ethnic identities as the occasion demands. Although fullbloods are perhaps not burdened with the psychological conflicts seemingly inherent in an unstable ethnic identity, they are not afforded the social and economic advantages of a shifting identity.

Tribal laws and practices used to contain many provisions limiting the participation of minimal-blood-degree Cherokees in situations where a real Indian was needed. To be principal chief or vice chief, one-half Cherokee blood degree was required, and the same provision applied to the Miss Cherokee title. Even the Bureau of Indian Affairs typically provides scholarship money and other advantages only to Cherokees of at least one-fourth Indian blood degree. Maximal-blood-degree Cherokees thus took care to exclude minimal-blood-degree Cherokees from participation in certain aspects of Cherokee life. Other acts of exclusion are achieved covertly. And perhaps it is this exclusion, so greatly resented, which has served as the self-justification for minimal-blood-degree Cherokees' sometimes participation in white American society.

No matter what the cultural outlook or blood degree of an individual Cherokee is, however, there are economic advantages to identifying ethnically as a Cherokee Indian, and the most basic economic advantage is access to reservation land. Legally a corporation under North Carolina laws, the Eastern Band of Cherokee Indians' assets consist of its lands with the Band's members functioning as stockholders. Although reservation lands cannot be "owned," individual Band members can have possessory rights to tracts of land that can be sold to, bought from, willed to, or inherited from any other Band member. Access to land provides definite economic opportunities, especially since 1962.

These opportunities exist in spite of the fact that the reservation is too crowded and the land too poor and mountainous for large-scale farming. Because of conservationist concerns, lumbering likewise provides no steady income for someone with a tract of land. Even though the entire southern Appalachian region might be classified as poor, mountainous land, the Cherokees may have the worst of a worst area. Gulick describes the reservation as "second-best lands" and goes on to write that: "In terms of agricultural potential, there is little within the borders of the reservation to match the [white-owned] splendid bottom land section just west of the 3200-Acre Tract and other sections upstream along the Tuckasegee; nor is there anything to match the rolling terrain beginning just south of the ridge which forms the southern slopes of Soco Valley."[30]

But possessing Indian land does offer opportunities. The cheap price of reservation land, sometimes gotten for free if inherited, compares favorably with more expensive off-reservation land and high rents in nearby towns. Many Cherokees can survive more inexpensively by living in homes on the reservation and commuting long distances to find work than by moving closer to their off-reservation jobs. And, of course, since 1962 possessory rights to reservation land have given people the opportunity to acquire better homes through the Qualla Housing Authority.

So this basic tie to the land keeps white Indians and fullbloods in the area where they form factions and struggle with each other for political and economic power. Within the reservation white Indians largely possess the better lands that do exist, and this is resented by full-bloods.[31] Cherokee County tracts, for example, are less mountainous, less crowded, and more numerous than those in Graham County, even though the Graham County Indian population is larger.

So white Indians as a group have advantages over fullbloods: they hold possessory rights to the better reservation lands (better both for farming and for greater access to highways that bring millions of tourists into the area each summer). White Indians also can identify as Indian or white as the opportunities arise. But fullbloods as a group have an advantage over white Indians: they are exempt from the type of psychological stresses that are produced by a dual and ambivalent identity. French contrasts the self-image of traditionalist fullbloods with middle-class white Indians when he writes: "Prior to the current 'Indian Pride' (Pan-Indian) movement, the middle-class Cherokees were most susceptible to ambivalance regarding their self-image. This stemmed from the fact that they saw as their reference group the larger, white, middle-class culture, and they felt a 'negative' stigma of being Indian. This did not affect the conservative full-bloods as much since they had a strong sense of in-group solidarity channeled through the Harmony Ethic."[32] Because political power and economic benefits are also intertwined in the blood-degree factionalism among the Eastern Cherokees, it will probably continue to exist for a long time.

Factionalism certainly is not unique to the Eastern Cherokees. Many Native American communities have this problem, and there are probably few groups of people throughout the world who do not. There are, however, unique features to Eastern Cherokee factionalism. The often caste-like system of the south has placed social boundaries around groups where no significant cultural ones exist. Certainly both Indians and blacks within the south often have a core of cultural traits that have persisted despite acculturation, but frequently these groups are subjected to discriminatory practices when no overwhelming cultural differences can be cited as the cause for such discrimination. Sometimes whole groups are subject to these social boundaries, and sometimes only certain individuals within a group are. In the case of the Cherokees, minimal-blood-degree individuals can drift across boundaries, and even maximal-blood-degree Cherokees can do this more successfully than other southern ethnic groups such as non-reservation ("tri-racial") Indians, like the North Carolina Lumbees, and especially blacks. Social pluralism can continue to exist long after the disappearance of cultural pluralism. It is important to remember whether an ethnic group's persistence is the result of insiders' or outsiders' efforts, or both.

The Snowbird community presents an opportunity to analyze the behavior of a whole group of fullbloods, as opposed to focusing on the behavior of individual fullbloods. In fact, the political controversy described here permits an examination of a whole group of white Indians as well. To return to an earlier question, why should a whole community like Snowbird try so persistently to separate itself from white Indians? An answer may exist in comparing Snowbird to the other prominent Eastern Cherokee fullblood community in Big Cove, on the Qualla Boundary. Big Cove fullbloods are often portrayed, by both social scientists and the Cherokees themselves, as caught between two worlds and unable to deal with the realities of life. Snowbird fullbloods, on the other hand, are often perceived as adaptive and successful. Snowbird fullbloods may be categorized differently, not because they are less traditionalist than Big Cove but because politically Snowbird has had more opportunities to control directly its own destiny. The council controversy was so critical to Snowbird because it presented the dire possibility of Snowbird's ending up in exactly the same position as Big Cove: fullbloods and white Indians within the same political boundaries expending their energies every two years in an effort to control council seats and work in the interests of themselves and against the interests of the other faction. Until the council controversy, Snowbird was spared that time-consuming ordeal. For now, the Snowbird community seems to have worked out a de facto compromise with the Tomotla community rather than ever again have to face that kind of biennial political violence. Being secure in its political position within tribal government, especially before 1973, Snowbird was even free to attempt to manipulate white-dominated county government as well, offering the Indian community even more opportunities.

Behavior is not a type into which individuals or a whole community fit absolutely. Instead, behavior is dependent to a large degree on the demands of situations. Snowbird people are no more or no less real Indians than Big Cove people. They are both basically traditionalists, ascribing to the Harmony Ethic value system. They are also flexible, either succumbing to the frustrations of denied situations or rising to the opportunities of others. Snowbird could have lost a battle, but if the pattern of sharing the two council seats with Tomotla continues as a de facto agreement to have one councilmember apiece from each community, then Snowbird as a community and fullbloods as a group may maintain enough of their power, status, and autonomy within the Eastern Band.

4

A Ceremony

Overleaf: The bilingual cross of Little Snowbird Baptist Church illustrates the Snowbird community's bicultural adaptation, which includes both Christianity and older Cherokee traditions.
Photo by Ken Murray, 1990.

I HAVE ATTENDED SEVERAL TRAIL OF TEARS SINGINGS. In the early years, the singings were held along the banks of Snowbird Creek, later along Cornsilk Branch. The singing is held in June, a cool-weather, springtime month in Snowbird. The mood is joyous. Friday afternoon and evening is a time for reunions. For three days the Cherokee Nation is almost whole again; it almost continues to exist.

THE FIELD SETTING

The singing attracts dozens of Oklahoma Cherokees who flood back to their ancestral homeland in the East. Children play, singers set up equipment, and friends talk. Men haul pews outside from Zion Hill Baptist Church and set them among the lawn chairs so that more seats are available. But even with the church pews, the crowds are too large, and quilts are spread on the ground. After sunset people wrap themselves up in more quilts for warmth. Steam rises from coffee cups and hot dogs. Traditional Indian food like bean bread is served, too.

Group after group sings. Some are North Carolina Cherokees, and some are Oklahoma Cherokees. Some groups are white and from several different states. Whatever the group or language though, the emphasis is on the joyous music of Christianity, accompanied most frequently by electric guitars.

No moment is ever more thrilling for me than when, well after midnight, after all the guests have performed, the Snowbird Quartet takes the stage and sings "I'll Fly Away." Everywhere feet stomp to the music. The song always ends with a standing ovation. As with the Cherokee Nation, the membership of the Snowbird Quartet changes with each generation, but the quartet itself persists.

THE SIGNIFICANCE OF THE SITUATION

The ceremony called the Trail of Tears Singing began in Oklahoma in the 1950s. Cherokee Indians in one of the northeastern Oklahoma communities, descendants of those who survived the removal west over the Trail of Tears, started the annual ceremony. It lasts for several days each summer and takes place in a church. The Trail of Tears Singing in North Carolina, begun in 1968, is also conducted by Cherokee Indians, descendants of those who escaped the removal of 1838. It lasts for several days each summer and is held outdoors at a singing ground in the Snowbird community of Graham County.

The ceremony is named for the route, the Trail of Tears, over which approximately sixteen thousand Cherokee Indians were forcibly marched to Indian Territory (now Oklahoma) in the winter of 1838 and 1839. Removed from their homes at gunpoint and held in stockades for weeks or months, at least four thousand Cherokees died of disease, exposure, malnutrition, starvation, and murder during or immediately before the removal march. The death rate was particularly high among the children, and numerous deaths must have occurred every day of the march. The continual mourning christened the route the "Trail of Tears," a route lined with thousands of unmarked graves. The Trail of Tears is a real and a symbolic link between the two major populations of Cherokee Indians, those in North Carolina and those in Oklahoma. It is thus appropriate that two ceremonies that annually reunite the Cherokees should be named after the Trail of Tears. It is, after all, necessary for each group to retrace the trail in order to join the other body of people, and for the Cherokees in Oklahoma it is the path back to their ancestral homeland. The Trail of Tears serves as a reminder that the Cherokees, although in 1838 supposedly the most acculturated Indian group in the United States, were nevertheless Indians and subject to all the racist, discriminatory practices leveled at any Native American.

The Trail of Tears Singing in North Carolina is a direct result and one of the better examples of continued contact between Eastern and Western Cherokees. A Snowbird Cherokee minister, Reverend Ikey Jackson, attended the Western Cherokee ceremony as a visitor and was so inspired by the phenomenon that he resolved to begin a similar ceremony in the east, a goal he accomplished in 1968, four years before his accidental death. Since the creation of the Trail of Tears Singing ceremonies in the west and east, the ceremonies themselves have encouraged further contact between the separated Cherokees. One of the North Carolina organizers of the Trail of Tears Singing in the east, Clarence Jackson, Ikey Jackson's son, has described the ceremony as "one of the major ways that we stay in touch." Ever increasing numbers of Cherokees from Oklahoma travel to North Carolina in June or July for the ceremony. Then in August Cherokees from North Carolina travel to Oklahoma. One measure of the success of the Trail of Tears Singing in North Carolina is that it has inspired more groups of Snowbird Cherokees to organize similar

summer singings. In the summer of 1990, for example, three such sing-
ings were held, in addition to the Trail of Tears. I was able to attend the
Billy Fourkiller Memorial Singing organized by Edna Chickalilee and
named for an Oklahoma Cherokee singer who died in 1978. Oklahoma
Cherokees attended all these singings, and numerous North Carolina
Cherokees visit Oklahoma several times a year as well.

Two characteristics are most notable about the Cherokee participants
at each Trail of Tears ceremony: for the most part, they are fundamentalist Christians, and they are also fluent Cherokee-language speakers.
The first of these characteristics is indicative of their degree of acculturation and their identity with many Americans and especially their white
Appalachian neighbors. Because of this acculturation, the Trail of Tears
Singing is a good example of interethnic relations. The second characteristic symbolizes the degree to which Eastern Cherokees have retained
crucial Cherokee traits and identify as a Native American ethnic group
and with Western Cherokees. Because of this the singing is a good example of intertribal relations. At the Trail of Tears Singing it is possible
to observe Snowbird Cherokees interacting with people from other Eastern Cherokee communities, Eastern Cherokees in general interacting
with Western Cherokees, and Indians interacting with whites.

It is possible to make some general comparisons between Snowbird's
Trail of Tears Singing and the Qualla Boundary's Fall Festival. Both
present aspects of Cherokee traditionalism—for example, the Cherokee
language at the Trail of Tears Singing and crafts, dances, and stickball at
the Fall Festival. There are differences, however, if only that the crafts,
dances, and stickball games at the Fall Festival are often attempts to re-
vitalize such traditions for a younger generation of Cherokees who have
no personal experiences with such endeavors. By contrast, the traditionalism at the Trail of Tears Singing need not be orchestrated since the
Cherokee tongue is still a living language in Snowbird. The Cherokee
identity which comes across at the Trail of Tears Singing seems to me,
therefore, to be less contrived.

THE SITUATION

I will describe here the 1974 event, the second time I attended the
singing, as typical. During the 1974 singing as I drove from Ned Long's
family's home, where I was staying, to the ceremony that Friday evening,

I passed through several categories of land: Cherokee reservation lands, mostly divided up into one-family possessory holdings; national forests owned by the federal government; land privately owned by non-Indians; land privately owned by Indians; and lands, both reservation and non-reservation, upon which community buildings, mostly churches, were situated. I drove through each category of land more than once in the four or five miles of twisting mountain road which followed Snowbird Creek.

There were only a couple of hours of daylight left when I arrived at the singing ground. Just as the time before, the singing took place on the banks of Snowbird Creek in the open ground sandwiched among the local Bureau of Indian Affairs representative's home, Head Start day care school, community building, Snowbird Tech (for adult education), and Zion Hill Baptist Church. Since 1975 a new singing ground has been cleared nearby along Cornsilk Branch by the Trail of Tears Organization. But in 1974 the singing was among these buildings in the clearing near Snowbird Creek. Many local people say that close by, if not on that very spot, earlier generations of Indians held dances and chanted at a "stomp ground" used for ancient Cherokee ceremonies. Flint projectile points and pottery sherds have been found nearby.

Although clear, the weather was cool by sunset and became progressively colder as the singing lasted until well after midnight. For warmth people in the audience wore kerchiefs, hats, sweaters, and coats over their work clothes. By contrast, most of the singing groups were quite well dressed as they performed atop the outdoor stage. Many of the women singers, especially whites, wore identical, elegant, floor-length gowns.

The stage was built of wooden planks by men of the community. By the first night of the event, it had been covered with black tar-paper, and in yellow paint across the front was written, "Welcome to the Trail of Tears Gospel Singing." Speaker systems, microphones, other electronic equipment, and a piano cluttered the stage, on either side of which two posts with a wire strung between them supported several lights. To the right of the stage, between it and the community building, stood a yellow cart for hauling the singers' equipment and a yellow van belonging to one of the singing groups. To the left stood the swingset of the Head Start school. In a semicircle in front of the stage, pews from Zion Hill Baptist Church, folding chairs, and lawn chairs had been casually arranged on the freshly cut grass. Only a few feet behind the stage Snowbird Creek flowed and behind that were thick forests and high mountains. Many people stood off to the sides or behind the pews since there were not enough seats for everyone present. Some sat or stood among the trees along the hillside that separated the front of the clearing from the narrow dirt road. Children played among the crowd, and at any one time during the three-day event nearly a dozen children could be seen playing on the large Head Start school sliding board.

The event had a more casual atmosphere than any of the monthly Sunday singings I had attended at either Indian or non-Indian area churches. The children playing, everyone dressed in work or school clothes, and the people eating and drinking snacks lent to the gathering a more relaxed social atmosphere not found inside the churches. The fact that each singing group was applauded after its performance and many were interrupted with applause also differed markedly from what occurred inside the churches during the monthly Sunday singings. There also seemed to be a greater emphasis on the singing ability of each performer than on the message of his song. At the monthly church singings it is typical for a performer to say that how well he sings is of little importance compared to the lesson his song teaches. But outside at the annual Trail of Tears Singing, groups were requested to do songs in which the whole range of a singer's ability could be tested and aesthetically rated. Groups knew how well the audience rated them by the number of times they were interrupted by applause and also by the number of amateur photographers who came forward to snap their pictures. Spontaneous preaching, a frequent and often lengthy occurrence at the monthly church singings, was limited at the Trail of Tears Singing to occasional phrases of praise, prayer, and thanksgiving.

By far the largest crowd during the three-day singing gathered on Saturday. Most of the bus loads of Western Cherokees from Oklahoma had not been able to complete their journey until then. More white singing groups from neighboring states also arrived, and again crowds of people from the local white community, other Eastern Cherokee communities on the main reservation (fifty miles from Snowbird), and, of course, members of the Snowbird Cherokee community all arrived early in the afternoon to begin the festivities. Snowbird Cherokees were outnumbered by Eastern Cherokees from other communities, and all the Indians present were overwhelmingly outnumbered by whites. One of the organizers of the Singing, Clarence Jackson, estimated the number of the crowd Saturday night at between fifteen hundred and two thousand people ("It's growed every year"), and another local Cherokee man, Gilliam Jackson, estimated the percentage of whites at 65 percent of the total. The total Snowbird population was then only about 320 in a total county population (Indian and white) of about 6,000. The total Eastern Cherokee population was then about 7,000, and Western Cherokees were more than twice as numerous. The hosts for the Trail of Tears Singing, the Snowbird Indian community, were, therefore, out-numbered by many categories of guests. Thus, the Trail of Tears Singing is a good example of one of the many activities numerically dominated by other groups in which Snowbird successfully participates, even occasionally assuming a leadership role.

The clearing by Snowbird Creek was crammed with Indians and whites, men and women, young and old. The church pews bulged with people, and on Saturday even more people had to stand than on Friday. Whites talked with Indians seated near them on the long pews, and efforts to appraise the singing groups encouraged Western and Eastern Cherokees and Indians and whites to chat. Several groups of people spread quilts or tablecloths on the ground and sat on these. In the warm summer weather the atmosphere was almost that of a carnival. Inside the community building food was busily being prepared, bought, and eaten to benefit the Trail of Tears Organization—food that included coffee, soft drinks, hot dogs, hamburgers, pastries, and a Cherokee specialty, bean bread. At the other end of the open ground, similar food items were being sold by members of the Snowbird Rescue Squad in their building to benefit their organization. Outside, all traffic control at the singing was in the hands of squad members. Over cups of coffee and pieces of bean bread, people from the diverse groups renewed old friendships or began new ones.

The community building, where most of the food was being prepared, contains a large meeting room with tables and chairs, a spacious kitchen, and bathrooms. In the meeting room hang two paintings, done by the local BIA representative's daughter, of an Indian in buckskin clothing and long hair killing a bear on the bank of a stream and another of an older Snowbird Cherokee woman sitting beside a mortar and pestle, a woman who in reality is Maggie Axe Wachacha, the former Indian (language) Clerk for Tribal Council and a sometime Indian doctor. The same woman, who speaks no English, attended the three-day singing wearing her gray hair tied up in the traditional red Cherokee women's kerchief, which she also wore in the painting. At any time during the singing other older women, all wearing the red kerchiefs and none an English-speaker, could be seen wandering among the crowd or sitting and listening to the music.

Just outside the community building a canvas canopy had been erected by a white singing group whose members were busily selling sheet music and record albums of their songs. All of the items for sale were neatly arranged on a table covered with a white cloth. Near the canopy stood a huge old red-and-white bus emblazoned on its sides with "Millionaire Quartet—Crusade for Jesus" and on its front merely with "Millionaire." It belonged to one of the out-of-state white singing groups. Next to it were the vans and cars of other singing groups. Near one van a group of whites sat on a tablecloth spread on the ground. Children played tag, running around the vehicles. Behind the cars, on the shady hillside, many people stood or sat and listened to the music.

At the other end of the open ground, near the rescue squad building, the parking area was full of cars, trucks, trailers, vans, campers, and tents. Beside the campers and pitched tents, lawn chairs had been arranged by those who would be camped along the bank of Snowbird Creek for the duration of the singing.

Since Friday evening the stage area had become more cluttered. As more and more groups arrived with their own electronic gear and instruments, some of the equipment was shifted from the top of the stage to a position in front of it with some of the gear partially blocking the welcome sign.

On Saturday several of the groups that had performed on Friday sang again, together with many new groups, especially those from Oklahoma. Once again the singing did not break up until well after midnight. The white singing groups, whether local or from out-of-state, seemed more elaborately dressed than either the North Carolina or Oklahoma Cherokee groups. With few exceptions all the women in white groups wore identical floor-length gowns, and the men almost always wore identical coats and ties.

Occasionally the singers in a white group were not all dressed similarly, and occasionally this was also true of an Indian group. But even when the singers in an Indian group were all dressed alike, the women usually wore knee-length dresses, and the men seldom wore coats and ties. In one Oklahoma Cherokee quartet, for example, the two women wore green knee-length dresses, and the two men wore green shirts with black trousers but no coats or ties. Performing Saturday night, an Oklahoma Cherokee trio were attired in identical red-checked dresses with white "Indian vests" with red fringe for the two women singers and white trousers and a red-checked shirt with red "Indian fringe" across the front and back for the man.

Although that group's clothing basically followed an American style, their outfits were modified slightly to look more Indian. I had seen something similar at the annual Fall Festival on the main reservation where local Cherokee clogging groups wore fringed clothing, moccasins, and headbands, or had their hair in braids in order to look more Indian. At both the Fall Festival and Trail of Tears Singing these performing groups were attempting to look more Indian while practicing a non-Indian style of singing or dancing. In the group of spectators, at both the Trail of Tears Singing and Fall Festival, a few teenagers and younger adults could be seen wearing bits of Indian attire. One younger man at the Trail of Tears Singing wore a beaded neck choker with ornaments dangling down from it. Even older Indians could occasionally be seen wearing Indian "corn bead" (Job's tears beads) necklaces or other types of beaded necklaces, for the women, or beaded "neckties," for the men. Many older women, as noted, wore the traditional women's kerchief. One major difference between the Fall Festival and the Trail of Tears Singing is that recently the Fall Festival also presented groups performing traditional, pre-Christian Cherokee dances and chants which are being revived, such as the booger, horse, and beaver dances.

The most striking characteristic about the Indian singers, whether from Oklahoma or North Carolina, however, was not how they dressed but how they sang. Almost every Indian group sang some of its selections in the Cherokee language. The songs were standard gospel tunes, such as "Amazing Grace," but they were sung in Cherokee. Since the music was the same, even whites totally unfamiliar with the language knew the song being sung. In addition, in singing gospel songs in Cherokee the tonal quality of the spoken language disappears, and the Cherokee language is "Anglicized" and made to sound less "foreign" to those more accustomed to English. Many groups alternated languages, singing one verse of a song in English and then the same verse in Cherokee. Local whites, who do not speak any Cherokee but have become familiar with some of the lines of Cherokee versions of songs through repetition, would occasionally request a Cherokee version of a song by shouting out the first line in Cherokee to a group on stage. There was at least one North Carolina Cherokee group whose lead singer, a woman, does not speak the Cherokee language but has learned most of the Cherokee versions of popular songs through repeatedly hearing them sung. Many local whites think she speaks Cherokee (and she never tells them that she does not). Most Indian singing groups at the Trail of Tears Singing, however, could speak as well as sing in Cherokee. Since they must usually converse with whites as well as Indians when they perform, most also speak English.

When the Oklahoma Cherokee group with the fringed outfits performed Saturday night, repeated interruptions of applause attested to their popularity. The appeal of their Indian costumes was evident from the number of amateur photographers, both Indian and white, who rushed forward to snap their pictures.

As the warm Saturday afternoon blended into a cold night, more sweaters, coats, kerchiefs, and hats, including a couple of cowboy hats from Oklahoma, appeared in the crowd. People bundled themselves up in massive quilts and huddled on the ground or crowded together on the church pews. As little Indian girls moved through the crowd selling chances on an Indian-made quilt to benefit the Trail of Tears Singing, the cold weather and the prospect of a warm quilt probably prompted many to buy a raffle ticket.

That evening two white men, leaders of out-of-state singing groups, took over the stage for about a half hour in order to collect money to support the Trail of Tears Organization. They requested that the male singers from each group come forward to pick up cardboard boxes to pass around through the crowd for donations. Their very non-Indian technique for collecting money was direct and assertive: "You fellows, you might as well grab your boxes or something because we got to shake some money, from somewheres. . . . Now, who's going to be first to give us a five-dollar bill?"

While the collection was going on, members of the Snowbird Indian Quartet stood quietly watching from the back of the stage. Although a quartet, the group sometimes grows to five members when, on special occasions like the Trail of Tears Singing, a former member returns to sing with the group. Two of the regular members of the group are brothers, Raymond and Clarence Jackson, the sons of Trail of Tears Singing founder Ikey Jackson, and they are key members of the Trail of Tears Organization and handle most of the master-of-ceremonies duties at the singing.

The Snowbird Quartet is by far the most popular singing group from the Snowbird community. It is better organized than the informal groups who occasionally sing at the monthly Sunday church events. I have yet to attend a monthly church singing at which the Snowbird Quartet did not sing, and when they sing, they must fulfill many requests. Although the group has genuine singing talent plus the ability to use electric guitars and sound equipment, at first they do not appear as professional as other singing groups who invest in uniform stage clothes. I have never seen the group appear at an event, even the Trail of Tears Singing, dressed uniformly or wearing coats and ties. Nevertheless, the group is most popular and is invited to sing at neighboring white as well as Indian churches.

This visiting in each other's churches on singing days is one of the main sources of voluntary contact between local whites and Indians. One of the first white-Indian marriages in the Snowbird area, that of Ned and Shirley Long, occurred as a result of the couple's meeting at a church singing.

The present Snowbird Quartet is not the first Snowbird Quartet ever to be organized. The first one included the father of two of the present members. With one exception, all the members of the first group are dead. The Snowbird Quartet as a name and tradition is probably the oldest singing group in the Snowbird community. Despite shouts from the audience calling upon the Snowbird Quartet to appear on stage, the group displayed traditional Indian modesty, and both Friday and Saturday nights the group performed last, after every guest group had performed. Perhaps because of the quartet's popularity, crowds remained at the Trail of Tears Singing until well after midnight when the Snowbird Quartet finally appeared, singing in both English and Cherokee.

The third day of the Trail of Tears Singing began on a sunny, warm Sunday afternoon immediately after church services. Several of the out-of-state singing groups had visited local churches that morning to sing or preach before driving over to the Trail of Tears Singing. Again there was a large crowd of spectators in the clearing by Snowbird Creek, and the church pews and lawn chairs were full of people. Many stood or sat off to the sides of the stage among the trees lining the creek or on the shady hillside between the road and the front of the clearing.

One major feature of the crowd differed from those of the two previous days. Everyone who had the means was quite well dressed. People wore their best church clothes, and some wore the best clothes they owned. Two sisters-in-law, for example, were wearing the beautiful, expensive outfits they had purchased a few months earlier for one's father's funeral. Everyone was not so well dressed, but hardly any woman or girl could be seen wearing slacks or jeans. Many men still were not wearing coats and ties, but few were dressed in their work clothes either. Older Indians were not as stylishly dressed as their children or grandchildren, many women still wearing the traditional red kerchief.

As people wandered around through the crowd, they passed groups who continued for the third day selling record albums and sheet music. A green "Gospel Singer" van and a yellow "Gospel Jubileers" van displayed records for sale. Sales of food in the community building also continued until late afternoon. Cars still packed the parking area, though all the tents had been packed away, and vehicles were parked along both sides of the narrow dirt road leading into the singing area.

Gradually, as Sunday lengthened and people began to think about the long drives home that preceded the Monday work day, the crowds thinned, and the Trail of Tears Singing came to an end for another year. As I also left and drove through Robbinsville, Graham's county seat, on my way home to Chapel Hill, I saw signs still visible in white-owned shop windows which read "The 7th Annual Trail of Tears Gospel Singing beginning 7 p.m. Friday Night June 28, 1974," evidence of the money brought into the area from visitors to the singing.

THE ANALYSIS

Unlike the political controversy previously described, the Trail of Tears Singing largely represents the favorable side of intercommunity relations. Snowbird Cherokees comprise a small community of only about 380 people. Despite their minority status both within and outside of the Eastern Band of Cherokee Indians, however, Snowbird people often play leadership roles in situations involving more than just the Snowbird community.

The council controversy demonstrated the community's desire to maintain a leadership role within tribal government. One of the resentments voiced by a main reservation white Indian against Snowbird during that controversy was that Snowbird "takes care of itself" by manipulating the Graham County government structure and therefore does not need so much power in tribal government. It is surprising how successful the tiny Snowbird community sometimes is in dealing simultaneously with county and tribal governments, but it is doubtful that Snowbird can be said actually to manipulate groups which vastly outnumber the community. Positions of authority or prominence held by Indians within Graham County include vice chair of the county's Democratic Party, a position on a four-county advisory board, president of the Robbinsville Athletic Association, law enforcement officers on the county's police force, jurors in court trials, star athletes on school basketball and football teams, organizers of amateur softball teams that include both Indian and white players, and employees of the county's federally funded Mainstream program.

The last position is interesting because some Snowbird people were at the time also employees of the tribe's federally funded Mainstream program, demonstrating how Snowbird managed to involve itself in two projects when most communities could qualify for participation in only one. The Indian deputies represented a different method of tapping two resources. The deputies worked for the county in both Indian and non-Indian communities but were paid from funds controlled by the Eastern Band. (The police force in Graham County was exclusively white until the two Indian deputies were hired.) One position in particular, vice chair of the local Democratic Party, was not the result of Snowbird's influence but resulted from implementation of the McGovern guidelines in 1972 which required equal representation of all ethnic groups, ages, and sexes. Two of the Snowbird men who have held the position of vice chair are former tribal councilmembers, one of whom has contemplated running for a county commissioner seat and was appointed to a four-county advisory board.

Most of the positions listed above are examples of successful efforts to have two ethnic groups interact equally within the same institutions. There are, however, also institutions of separation, mostly the churches, in which the membership is from one ethnic group or the other. Both white churches and Indian churches, however, have numerous singings throughout the year. Whichever group comprises the membership of the church acts as host, even if the guests vastly outnumber the church membership, which is often the case for Indian churches. At the Trail of Tears Singing, the entire Snowbird community, not just the organizers of the singing, was outnumbered by its guests. This condition was not resented but welcomed, since one of the main purposes of the singing was for Christians of any ethnic group to join together. The feeling that people should view the singing mainly as a gathering of Christians and not only as an Indian event was voiced in an interview with a young Snowbird man at the singing who resented those whites who did not view Indians as the spiritual equals of whites and who acted paternalistically toward Indians: "[Whites] would say . . . the Indians are going to have their big deal, have the big singing, something like even the attitude of our Indians can do this, whereas, you know, I don't like that kind of attitude. . . . You know, maybe they could say our brothers or our sisters are planning their annual thing. And nobody's bitter about it. It's, you know, something about that can be overlooked." As a gathering of Christians, the Trail of Tears Singing is symbolic of the Cherokees' degree of acculturation and their identity with many Americans and their white Appalachian neighbors. Whites reinforced this image Snowbird has of itself by turning out in large numbers to view or participate in the singing; an estimated 65 percent of those there were whites. Contributions of money to the Trail of Tears Organization by whites also supported this image.

In a different context, the large turnout of Western Cherokees and people from other Eastern Cherokee communities reinforced Snowbird's image of itself as a real Indian community. In that sense the Trail of Tears Singing is symbolic of the degree to which the community possesses crucial Cherokee traits and identifies as a Native American ethnic group. The 1838 removal over the Trail of Tears was a stark reminder to the Cherokees that no matter how acculturated they became they were still Indians. Otherwise they would never have been removed west. The modern Trail of Tears Singing likewise emphasizes the dual identity of a people involved in both acculturation and persistence.

Robert E. Daniels has said of the Sioux that "their major significance in American life lies in history."[1] Just as the Sioux speak of the Battle of the Little Big Horn and the Wounded Knee Massacre, so the Cherokees speak of the Trail of Tears. The use of the Cherokee language by Indian singing groups at the Trail of Tears Singing was the most obvious way

in which Indianness was demonstrated. The presence of Indian clothing and jewelry and occasional Cherokee food items, like bean bread,
however, was also a means of asserting a Native American identity. The
large turnout of Oklahoma Cherokees, a larger group, according to the
organizers, than those in attendance from any other one state except
North Carolina confirmed that the event was an Indian affair, despite
other purposes the gathering served.

In many ways Snowbird is an appropriate place for a gathering
at which Indianness is asserted. Snowbird has a high percentage of
Cherokee-language speakers, fullbloods, native craftsmen, and Indian
doctors. It is therefore a real Indian community and an appropriate place
for a real Indian ceremony. As one of those interviewed at the Trail
of Tears Singing explained, in response to a question about whether
the event was more Christian or Indian: "It's probably a combination
of both. In the sense that most of the Indians around here, they will
go to the mountain to pray . . . and it gives them sort of a different
feeling . . . and I imagine in that sense . . . it's similar to it here tonight."
Snowbird's practice of occasionally holding religious events outdoors, a
habit associated with Indianness, was cited as an example of how one
Cherokee community maintained its Indian traditions.

There may also be practical reasons why events similar to the Trail
of Tears Singing are not held in other Eastern Cherokee communities.
There are at least three annual major Indian events held within the
Eastern Cherokee area: Indian Day, held on the main reservation in
mid-spring before the tourist rush begins each year; the bigger Fall Festival, held on the main reservation in mid-autumn after the tourist rush
ends; and the Trail of Tears Singing, held during the summertime tourist
onslaught but in a community hardly affected at all by tourism. A ceremony such as the Trail of Tears Singing probably could not be held on the
main reservation during the summer and successfully exclude tourists
from participating. Summer, the vacation season, is a convenient time
for getting people together and certainly a time of year when mountain
roads are free of ice and snow and easy to travel. There are, therefore,
advantages to a summer event that are further maximized by holding
the event in a more remote community like Snowbird. Snowbird is thus
able to hold a ceremony at which Indian identity is expressed during a
season when other Eastern Cherokee communities are not in as much of
a position to do so.

The Trail of Tears Singing is, however, not only a vehicle for the expression of tribal and intertribal identity. It is also a major event for the voluntary association of local whites and Indians, for interethnic relations. For more than a century and a half the land distribution pattern in the Graham County area has meant Indians and whites have had intense, and usually harmonious, relations. Unlike the Qualla Boundary where there are two large blocks of land, the thirteen small blocks of Snowbird reservation land are interspersed nearly checkerboard style with white-owned tracts. For over a century it has been virtually impossible for Snowbird Cherokees to live in isolation from non-Indians. Until the post–World War II tourist boom, many Cherokees on the main reservation were able to maintain such isolation. Because of its long history of relations with non-Indian communities, Snowbird is thus an appropriate location for an event like the Trail of Tears Singing that brings whites and Indians together. That Snowbird should bring together both Indian and white communities at a single event is symbolic of Snowbird's dual identity, with tribe and fellow Band members and with county and non-Indian neighbors.

Although the avowed purpose of the Trail of Tears Singing is religious, the event has other obvious aims. It is to a large extent also a social event that provides a scene for family reunions and the meeting of old friends, and an occasion for children to play and adults to eat out and be entertained by good music. The more casual dress of much of the crowd, the rambunctious play of the children, outbursts of applause and laughter, and little need to pay close attention to the events on stage all emphasize the purely social context of the event, in contrast to the more orderly monthly Sunday church singings. One of the singing's organizers described the event as "entertainment" and suggested that people came to the gathering because they were "gospel music lovers." One of the singers in a white group said, "Everybody gets here looking for a great time," and another white man described the singing as a "social get-together."

All this is not to say that a religious message is lacking, but the organizers, performers, and audience depend upon the songs to get the spiritual message across rather than looking to sermons or lengthy testimonials. Even when efforts at witnessing occur, it is usually as a short introduction to a song.

Aside from its spiritual purpose and its function as entertainment, the Trail of Tears Singing has, for some people, an economic advantage. The concentrated effort to collect money to perpetuate the Trail of Tears Organization has already been mentioned. In addition, individual singing groups sell albums of their music to the large crowd making the event, for some, a money-making affair. Also, as one of the men who encouraged the audience to contribute to the Trail of Tears Organization said, "These [singing] groups, you know, a lot of you got enough [future] bookings out of this that it'll really help you out [financially]. You ought to be able to give five or ten dollars." Local businesses also profited by the large crowds. When one white store owner was asked if the singing helped business, she replied enthusiastically, "It sure does."

A whole network of gospel singing groups is spread throughout the southeastern United States, and, as a group's contacts within the network expand, the number of engagements the group has increases. Money collections at church singings or revivals almost always pay a group at least for its travel expenses. Groups are recruited for the Trail of Tears Singing when the event's organizers, as part of a singing group, tour the countryside. One of the organizers could have been explaining the concept of reciprocity when he said: "You know, the Snowbird Indian Quartet? They go from place to place to sing, and they're the ones that draws the crowds in here, and they're the ones that works with these groups. . . . They [the singing groups] come in here once a year. Then year by year we go out and help them. . . . that's the reason they come to help us. So that's how we stay in contact with these people. And the western Indians, we go out there to their Trail of Tears Gospel Singing."

The Trail of Tears Singing was inspired by and came into being through the efforts of one Snowbird Cherokee man, Ikey Jackson, a charismatic leader and an entrepreneur in Fredrik Barth's sense.[2] An innovative man who turned to preaching late in life, Jackson actively sought answers to the conflicting values dominating his own life. Before the Trail of Tears Singing, the Eastern Band of Cherokee Indians were geographically isolated from other Native American groups and were often slow in learning of and identifying with the concerns of other Indians. As a major way in which Eastern Cherokees stay in touch with other groups, the Trail of Tears Singing should assist in changing the attitudes and values of the Eastern Band by diminishing the importance of their physical isolation. Barth suggests that, "Entrepreneurial activity thus tends to make a bridge between what before was separated."[3] Through the Trail of Tears Singing two factions from two distinct Indian groups have found they share a common appreciation for Indian traditionalism. The event is perpetuated each year by the efforts of the founder's two sons and others in the community. It fulfills a dual purpose: it is a moving, musically religious event that people from diverse communities attend, and it is a major means of contact between the Eastern and Western Cherokees, separated for more than a century and a half and by several hundred miles. Only a small group, about twenty people associated with the founder's church, Zion Hill Baptist, act as the Trail of Tears Organization and begin the planning of each year's event. By the time the Trail of Tears Singing takes place, however, participants include nearly the entire Snowbird community, other Eastern Cherokees, Western Cherokees from Oklahoma, and whites from both the local area and several surrounding states.

Whites who participate may have never before seen an Indian or may have grown up near Snowbird with Cherokee neighbors. If any non-Indian participants harbor prejudices against Indians, those feelings are usually well concealed during the course of the event. Out-of-state whites, who attend in large numbers, may in fact be neutral in their feelings toward Indians simply because they have had hardly any contact with Native Americans before the event. The manner in which the singing is conducted reinforces positive attitudes toward Indians. As one exuberant white singer said, "We love North Carolina; we love the Indians here. . . . We would rather sing in North Carolina than any place we ever sang." Whites who come from areas where prejudices against blacks are all too evident may lack similar feelings toward Indians with whom they have had no experience and do not compete for jobs.

Even local whites who do harbor negative feelings toward Indians tend to express those attitudes more subtly than anti-black feelings are expressed throughout much of the south. Since there is much for local whites to appreciate in the Trail of Tears Singing, the situation should further work to improve white-Indian relations. The event is a major source of entertainment in which whites as well as Indians can become involved. Religious convictions expressed during the singing are shared by both whites and Indians and reinforce common bonds between the two groups. Many local whites also benefit economically, as do some out-of-state whites, the influx of people increasing business for grocery stores, cafés and restaurants, gasoline stations, and motels, all of which are owned and operated by whites. Out-of-state white singing groups find a ready market for their record albums and make future bookings for other singings. When asked if the event had changed relations between Indians and non-Indians, one of the singing's organizers replied: "I think it's changed for the better myself. . . . We're amazed what kind of support we get from the non-Indians here in our community, in the surrounding counties, and surrounding states."

If the singing reinforces common religious bonds between Indians and whites and benefits economically many whites, it also improves white-Indian relations to the advantage of Indians as well as whites. The common religious bonds that the two groups share may be expressed, but they are expressed in a uniquely Indian way, through the medium of the Cherokee language. Diversity and commonality are expressed in the same act of singing "Amazing Grace" in the Cherokee language. These same qualities are expressed in the large cross at the Little Snowbird Baptist Church playground. Across the horizontal timber is written in English: "The Lord is My Shepherd." Across the vertical beam the same message is written in the syllabary of the Cherokee language. Whites hear their own views voiced via Cherokee-language versions of the gospel songs, but in a different style, and perhaps they grow more tolerant toward an Indian type of diversity. What Daniels has said of the Sioux could be applied to Cherokee communities like Snowbird: the group's concern is "with demonstrating the distinct position of an [Indian] social unit *within* the larger sphere of American society."[4]

If some whites may not be fully accepting of Indians and their ways, some Cherokees are not totally pleased with whites' attitudes. One young Cherokee man regretted that many whites viewed the singing only as an "Indian thing" and never as a Christian event that happened to be produced by the Indian segment of the population. Largely, however, the event does seem to improve white-Indian relations more than it hinders them.

Aside from the probable improvement of white-Indian relations, the event also functions to improve and maintain relations between Eastern and Western Cherokees. Although many people throughout the Eastern Cherokee reservation say that the Cherokee dialect spoken in Snowbird is "closer" than that of the main reservation to the dialect spoken in Oklahoma, there are still differences in the two versions of the Cherokee

language. Snowbird Cherokees and Oklahoma Cherokees speak variations of the Atali dialect while Qualla Boundary Cherokees speak the
Kituhwa dialect, often said by Eastern Cherokees themselves to be less
pure and distinct than Atali. Because the Oklahoma version of Cherokee with which Eastern Cherokees are familiar is said to resemble Atali
more than Kituhwa, it seems appropriate to have an intertribal event
like the Trail of Tears Singing at Snowbird, an Atali-speaking community. There are communications problems, however, as described by a
Western Cherokee: "We understand each other here in North Carolina.
They talk a little bit different than we do, but it all still means the same
deal, you know. . . . It's just a different pronunciation than we have because we got the real Cherokee language in Oklahoma." And an Eastern
Cherokee added: "We have a little trouble understanding each other.
They got . . . a little different sound to their Indian language. Some of
them you have to listen pretty close before you can understand it." The
Western Cherokee gave the following interesting, but unlikely, reason
for the dialect differences: "They said a long time ago when the Cherokees were driven from this area, they took the full-speaking Cherokees
to Oklahoma. So the people here that hid out in the mountains, well,
they just picked up what they could pick up [of the language]."

The same two individuals have both been primary in developing and
maintaining the two Trail of Tears Singings and have each made numerous visits to Oklahoma and North Carolina. Their observations of each
other's area, and each's obvious greater satisfaction with his own area
is interesting. The Western Cherokee says of the Eastern Cherokees:
"According to the history, the Cherokees in the west, in Oklahoma,
are more or less more advanced than the Eastern Band . . . We are
not on a reservation there. We live just like the white people there in
Oklahoma." And the Eastern Cherokee says of the Western Cherokees:
"Their working conditions are not like ours here in North Carolina. I
think our Indian farming is a little difficult for them over there. So we
have better opportunities . . . here in North Carolina." Although almost
all out-of-state white singing groups found their own lodging in motels
or campgrounds, probably all Western Cherokees, whether singers or
not, were housed in Eastern Cherokees' homes, demonstrating the close
ties felt between the two Cherokee groups. When asked if the Trail
of Tears Singing was important in maintaining ties between the two

groups, one of the organizers said, "That's one of the major ways that we stay in touch."

There are no political or legal ties joining Eastern and Western Cherokees, and the federal government has officially viewed them as two distinct groups since 1886. They live too far away from each other (and have for more than a century and a half) to maintain any sort of intense relations, which is reflected by the differing dialects of Cherokee that they speak. However, they do share a common language and a common religion. The two Cherokee groups also share a common respect for fullbloodedness and real Indianness, native craftsmen, practitioners of Indian medicine, and other symbols of Indian traditionalism. The Trail of Tears Singing symbolically reunifies the Cherokee people in their ancestral homeland. This is a major theme of the Trail of Tears Singing that is manifested each time a Cherokee group, whether from Oklahoma or North Carolina, takes the stage and begins to sing, as the Cherokees say, "in Indian." The event is a harmonious reuniting of the Cherokee Nation, especially those segments that view themselves as real Indians distinct from the white Indians in their midst in both the west and east.

The Trail of Tears Singing in the Snowbird community is unique. One of the tiniest of the Eastern Cherokee communities hosts the entire Cherokee Nation without the assistance of any other Cherokee community. One of the smallest Graham County communities hosts the rest of the county with no formal assistance from its non-Indian neighbors. In fact, non-Indians from half a dozen states show up as guests of the Snowbird community. The event expresses the harmonious aspects of Snowbird's relations with other groups of people. Other Eastern Cherokees, Western Cherokees, and non-Indians all participate, but Snowbird is in charge.

The event allows all of the Snowbird community's different identities to emerge, not as compartmentalized characteristics but as characteristics thoroughly blended together. In some ways the singing is comparable to similar events among other Indian groups, such as the Oglala Sioux Sun Dance, where "the sentiments of Sioux Nationalism are given their fullest expression: the Oglalas are fully American while continuing to be distinct."[5] The dual identities of each Snowbird Cherokee as a Native American and as an American exist simultaneously within the same individual and are expressed, for example, in the act of singing a gospel tune in the Cherokee language. The Trail of Tears Singing is an event that allows the harmonious expression of the dual identity of Snow-bird Cherokees to other Cherokees and to non-Indians. The event is not representative of the results of forced acculturation, cultural resistance, or personality conflict stereotypically associated with dual identity. It reflects and reinforces instead a more than adequately successful achievement of a community's dual identity.

The New World of Harmony

Overleaf: Women have always had influence in Cherokee matrilineal society. Ella Long Jackson, her two daughters, and a niece are typical in their commitment both to their families and to the larger community. Shown (left to right) are Ella Jackson, Shirley Jackson Oswalt, Brenda Long, and Lou Ellen Jackson Jones.
Photo by Ken Murray, 1990.

THE SNOWBIRD CHEROKEE COMMUNITY HAS, despite cultural changes, been successful in preserving its Native American ethnic identity as a traditionalist Cherokee Indian community. Compared to other Eastern Cherokee communities, Snowbird is quite traditional, even though neither the collective behavior of the group nor the behavior of individuals can always be considered typically culturally conservative.

Why Snowbird should be successful in preserving a core of real Indian traits while adapting so well to the world beyond the community is the question that has repeatedly presented itself to me. When I asked several Snowbird people this question, no one was able to come up with the concise simple explanation I initially hoped I would find for this complex problem. Perhaps my mistake was, as van Velsen has put it, "to assume, as many laymen do, that to be a member of a community is to understand it."[1] Although they certainly do not encompass the complete explanation, a few characteristics may begin to explain why Snowbird is simultaneously a traditional and an adaptive community.

Most importantly, the Snowbird community is relatively small, stable, and still to a great degree homogeneous. Kin ties of blood and marriage are important in achieving social cohesiveness, and in the absence of kinship there is the likelihood of stable, lifelong friendships, so rare in the rest of a highly mobile nation like the United States. The homogeneity of the Snowbird community is impressive in regard to blood degree, knowledge of the Cherokee language, religion, and financial condition, although it must be admitted that the percentage of both maximal-blood-degree Indians and Cherokee-language speakers is slowly declining. Snowbird's traditionalism hangs in a delicate balance, and this is unfortunate since the homogeneity based on traditionalism has minimized internal factionalism, which seldom surfaces in the community except in land disputes. All Snowbird residents are about equal in legal, political, and economic status, and they are culturally similar. As of the mid-1970s over 80 percent of the adult population was fullblood or nearly fullblood, and nearly 75 percent spoke the Cherokee language. (These percentages are even more impressive when one realizes that intermarried non-Indians were counted as community members.) There is even little difference in the economic situation, and in the 1970s more than half the families earned less than $5,000 annually and over three-fourths made less than $10,000. Only about 11 percent of the adult population were intermarried non-Cherokees, and only about 6 percent of the adults were Cherokees with one-half or less blood degree. Almost all the minimal-blood-degree Cherokees, who rarely participated in the affairs of the community, were isolated from the rest of Snowbird because they lived in the Mountain Creek area east of Robbinsville. In contrast, the fullbloods live west and southwest of Robbinsville in the Snowbird Creek area. Thus, the typical real Indian–white Indian factionalism that disrupts practically every other Eastern Cherokee community did not affect Snowbird until the council controversy with Tomotla in 1973. There were simply no major differences to generate opposed interest groups or factions.

Homogeneity has been a major factor contributing to the Snowbird community's adaptive success. White Indians are virtually non-existent in Snowbird. If intermarried non-Cherokees are excluded from consideration, the Snowbird community was in the mid-1970s more than 90 percent fullblood. This fact is all the more interesting when compared to the community of Big Cove, also characterized as a traditionalist community, and therefore the subject of most of the anthropological fieldwork conducted on the Eastern Cherokees in the last hundred years. Only about 30 percent of the Big Cove community was in the 1950s fullblood.[2] White Indians live in Big Cove, and their competition with real Indians for political power and ensuing economic advantages is well documented.

Ironically, many researchers have assumed Big Cove to be the ideal location for studying Cherokee traditionalists because the community is so physically isolated from whites. Big Cove is on the main reservation with other more accessible reservation communities buffering one side and the Great Smoky Mountains National Park on the other as insulation from the white world. Snowbird's scattered land holdings, on the other hand, have meant intense interaction with local whites over the decades. Therefore, Big Cove, the argument goes, should be more traditionalist than Snowbird since Big Cove is literally farther removed geographically from the white world.

The error in this assumption lies in the problem of correctly identifying the major elements of culture change and political and economic power over the last century. Whites, it can be argued, are not nearly so threatening to the survival of traditionalists as are white Indians. Snowbird traditionalists do not live in close proximity to white Indians; Big Cove traditionalists do. It may be an attractive explanation to attribute Big Cove's problems to a people under pressure to acculturate, "lost between two worlds," and retreating into the geographical isolation of the Big Cove community. Perhaps a more realistic explanation is that Big Cove traditionalists, unlike Snowbird traditionalists, have been denied any consistent access to political power through which they could manage their own lives and solve their own problems.

In fact, probably the main reason Snowbird fought the political merger with Tomotla into the Cheoah Township was to avoid a situation in which Snowbird would become intensely involved in local blood-degree factionalism, as is the case in Big Cove. Until the merger with Tomotla, Snowbird had not had to counterpose politically its real Indian identity against a specific white Indian community. Now that the two communities are merged into one political township, every biennial election for council could serve as a confrontation between the two groups like those that have occurred between fullbloods and white Indians in Big Cove for a century. Campaign strategies must be devised, and the best adaptive strategy that can probably be achieved is the election of one Cheoah councilmember from Tomotla and the other from Snowbird. Despite the political merger of the two communities into one township, however, the Snowbird Mountains and a county line physically separate the real Indian Snowbird community from the white Indian Tomotla community. This fact of geography plus the likely possibility of a long-term de facto compromise with Tomotla to split the two seats, a compromise which has been in effect for almost two decades, may work to preserve Snowbird's ethnic distinctiveness.

From traditionalists' point of view, white Indians, not local whites, today pose a real threat. Assuming Cherokee lands maintain their federal reservation status, local whites cannot seize the land of a traditionalist, have a say in land disputes, or rezone a possessory holding; nor can they share in Indian Claims Commission money or bingo profits; nor have a say in who gets access to low-cost housing; nor have access to Indian Health Service medical facilities. White Indians, on the other hand, can do all these things. Today real Indians and white Indians compete within the same ecological niche more than Indians as a group and local whites.

A secondary factor that explains Snowbird's simultaneous existence as a traditionalist and an adaptive community is its relative isolation from the heavy hand of outside white Bureau of Indian Affairs control. The BIA headquarters has always been located on the Qualla Bound-

ary where aspects of Indian life are in full view and sometime control
of government personnel. In Snowbird, however, there has never, for
example, been a BIA high school (although a day school existed until
1965), and now all Snowbird students attend county, not BIA, schools for
their entire educational lives. Located fifty miles from the main reservation, Snowbird historically has been isolated from the BIA's occasionally
arbitrary and authoritarian approach to Cherokee affairs.

An analogy can be made between contemporary Snowbird and the
entire pre-removal mountain region of the Cherokee country in the
early nineteenth century. The mountains were isolated from the white
onslaught that brought extensive acculturation to the more accessible
Cherokee hill country to the south, beyond the Snowbird Mountains.
The less contact an Indian community has had with the agents of acculturation, whether nineteenth-century missionaries or twentieth-century
BIA personnel, the less quickly that community has changed culturally
and ethnically and the less frequently it has been put in a paternalistic
relationship.

In describing the Oglala Sioux situation, Daniels has observed similar
circumstances and goes on to describe BIA employees and their goals:
"Even among the personnel of the local Bureau of Indian Affairs agency,
for whom the Oglalas are ostensibly the *raison d'etre*, the whites are in a
position of dominance which does not demand a general readjustment of
their concept to those of their wards and customers. The contact situation
has been defined for over a century as placing the burden of acculturation on the Sioux."[3] Many Indian communities have historically had
to bargain away their cultural traditions in order to obtain health care,
housing, food supplements, employment, and education that the federal
government dispenses. Indian individuals in full BIA view have had to
"shape up" and acculturate or lose valuable services. Snowbird is not
only apart from BIA view, but the community is not as dependent upon
the BIA for services as other Eastern Cherokee communities may be.

In fact, the whites with whom Snowbird people come in contact on a
daily basis are hardly the BIA personnel "in a position of dominance" in
relation to the community. Some Graham County whites may have more
money or a greater share of local political power than Snowbird people,
but most whites are not much better off in terms of income, education,
or political power, and certainly most do not have any direct authority
over the Indian community. Even the powerful white missionaries that

Daniels describes for the Pine Ridge Sioux Reservation do not exist in Snowbird. The few non-Indian missionaries who work with the Eastern Cherokees are almost all located on the Qualla Boundary, and three of Snowbird's four churches are in local Indian control. While native shamans may be attacked by white missionaries on the Sioux reservation, within Snowbird Cherokee churches "conjure men" are praised and sanctioned.[4] Thus, Snowbird may have been able to maintain more of its cultural traditions by being relatively isolated from the direct acculturating force of the BIA while simultaneously being in a position to manipulate and tap diverse sources for services (the tribe, county, state, and nation). This unique position has encouraged Snowbird's adaptive behavior.

Besides not being subjected to a white bureaucracy with superior income, education, and power, until recently Snowbird did not have to struggle intensely with a white Indian community for political representation within Tribal Council. Until recently, the community was virtually guaranteed two seats in Tribal Council and from this secure position could, if it chose, further manipulate the tribal political situation by allying with other fullbloods against the white Indian faction. Even now Snowbird will probably continue to hold one seat in council.

The variety of options and choices available to Snowbird, within the multiadaptive political situation in which it has existed for a century, has determined its strategic behavior. Snowbird has not had to depend exclusively on the Eastern Band, even during periods in which white Indians have held major political power. Likewise, it has not had to depend on the whims of a white federal BIA bureaucracy. Instead, Snowbird is increasing its involvement with Graham County. The whites there are in an economic condition similar to the Indians, even if they are culturally different. Importantly, unlike white Indians, whites pose no threats to Snowbird's Indian rights and status. Likewise, Snowbird's small population poses no threats to Graham County's white majority since Indians are only about 5 percent of the county's total population. Because of their small numbers, the Indians could never "take over" Graham County government or its services. Should local whites not cooperate with Snowbird in fulfilling the community's needs, however, Snowbird can continue to turn to the Eastern Band and the federal government.

The image that evolves of Snowbird is of a community with little internal strife because of its homogeneity, largely along traditionalist Eastern

Cherokee lines. An image also emerges of a community maintaining its autonomy by adapting to a variety of political and economic structures without becoming exclusively dependent upon any one of them.

Snowbird's real Indian ethnic identity is not threatened because it does no harm to the community in any of these contexts. It may even aid the group. Its real Indian identity allows the community to interact widely with Graham County and local whites without jeopardizing its Indian status, which is the unpleasant situation in which white Indians, who often look and act like whites, are placed when they interact intensely with white groups. Because they physically look Indian and live in a region of the country with a significant Indian population, most Snowbird people cannot deny their Indian identity. So they maximize the positive aspects of their Indianness. In other words, being traditionalist is usually not a handicap to adapting to the society of which the Snowbird community is a part. The two situations chosen for the extended case method, the 1973 political controversy and the Trail of Tears Singing, verify this view of Snowbird. Despite culture change, an Eastern Cherokee community like Snowbird does persist with a distinct ethnic identity as an Indian group. Despite adapting successfully to a variety of settings, including non-Indian ones, Snowbird continues to be thought of by Eastern Cherokees themselves as a very traditionalist community.

Van Velsen has singled out conflict situations as being especially appropriate for the extended-case method (situational analysis) used here: "The collection by the ethnographer of detailed data . . . implies the particular use to which such data are put in analysis, above all the attempt to incorporate conflict as a 'normal' rather than 'abnormal' part of social progress." Thus, the council controversy would seem an especially appropriate case for situational analysis. (The Trail of Tears Singing is a less appropriate subject for this method, but the data gathered from the event is needed to round out the image of the Snowbird community begun in analyzing the council controversy.) The controversy demonstrates how "norms . . . are ultimately manipulated by individuals in particular situations to serve particular ends."[5] Or, as Barth has explained: "[Patterns of behavior] are generated through processes of interaction . . . [that] reflect the constraints and incentives under which people act. . . . Values are evaluated, and on the basis of which choice is exercised."[6]

It obviously has been to the Snowbird community's best interests to preserve or secure as much power as possible within both the Eastern

Band and Graham County, the two areas of local government in which Snowbird has the greatest potential for direct representation. When the community's power within tribal government was threatened, Snowbird acted to minimize the threat. In meeting the threat Snowbird acted both traditionally and adaptively. The community's struggle in the council controversy revolved around the value it places on Indianness, which was manipulated as when fluent English-speakers repeatedly addressed Tribal Council in the Cherokee language, thus vividly demonstrating they were real Indians. On the other hand, the controversy gave incentives for Snowbird people to act in ways described by some as un-Indian, for example, more assertive behavior, such as utilizing the services of an attorney that placed the community in an adversarial situation. Interestingly though, traditional Cherokees are most likely to act aggressively in circumstances where the aggressive behavior is for the good of the group, as was the case in the council controversy. Thus, in attempting to manipulate events in the controversy, Snowbird experienced simultaneous incentives to act as Indians in regard to certain aspects of their behavior and to act unlike typical Indians in regard to other aspects. Snowbird people acted both traditionally and adaptively in the same situation. Tribal Council was a particularly appropriate background for witnessing both types of behavior since the Council contains both traditionalist (real Indian) members and more acculturated (white Indian) members.

At the Trail of Tears Singing, Snowbird people also simultaneously acted out two different roles. Again, by using the Cherokee language extensively, in both conversation and song, they demonstrated they were real Indians. Other symbols of Indianness were also utilized: some people wore Indian-style clothing; some ate bean bread, a traditional Cherokee food; and many people acted out typical harmony-oriented behavior, as when, despite repeated requests from the audience, the Snowbird Quartet would not perform until every other group had sung. The very name of the event, the Trail of Tears Singing, symbolizes a return to the ancestral homeland and a reuniting of Eastern and Western Cherokees. As Spicer indicates, the homeland and language signals are the most frequent symbols used by any group to emphasize ethnic identity.[7]

At the Trail of Tears Singing, however, Snowbird people also acted out roles other than the real Indian one. By inviting many white singing groups and their white neighbors, Snowbird people emphasized their unity with non-Indians. The fact that the singing was a Christian event using gospel music symbolized the community's oneness with its neighboring white Appalachian communities and the rest of America. Snowbird people were acting out two roles at once.

Thus, Snowbird exists as a traditionalist Cherokee community, despite its intense interactions with non-traditionalist Indian and non-Indian communities. Barth's ideas are particularly useful in answering why this condition should exist. He offers a generative model of social organization that represents a compromise in anthropological theory between cultural determinism and individual free will as the causes behind social phenomena.[8] Barth suggests that "the most simple and general model available to us is one of an aggregate of people exercising choice while influenced by certain constraints and incentives. . . . Our central problem becomes what are the constraints and incentives that canalize choices."[9] The preceding chapters have outlined two situations in which choices were made by the aggregate of Snowbird people, particularly during the council controversy, and indicated the constraints and incentives under which those people acted. These situations demonstrate that despite some cultural adaptation to the non-Indian world, the Snowbird community has consistently opted for its basically Indian status. Under what constraints and incentives did the Snowbird people act?

The constraints on Indianness revolve around three important patterns of behavior. To survive as a real Indian community, enough Snowbird individuals must choose to live in the *geographical* area, the homeland, as a visible reminder that the group survives; enough must choose to marry other Indians to thus preserve the *physical* dimensions of fullbloodedness; and enough must both choose to learn, habitually speak, and teach their children the Cherokee language and engrain in their children the values of the Harmony Ethic to thus preserve the major *cultural* dimensions of fullbloodedness. Individuals who do not learn the Cherokee language or prefer to speak English; who do not act Indian; who marry non-Indians, white Indians, or even non-Cherokee-speaking fullbloods; and who permanently leave the area risk losing for themselves and their descendants their Indian status. There is probably a greater chance of someone losing an Indian identity if any or all of these characteristics apply: being raised in a household with some non-Indian members, especially a parent; marrying a non-Indian, especially one not interested in Indianness; learning only English, and thereby being excluded from events where only Cherokee is spoken; and receiving the type of education that does not prepare one for local employment but does lead to a well-paying job in a distant area.

Incentives do operate to maintain a status of real Indianness. Although psychological needs are met by maintaining such a status, economic and physical needs suffice to provide adequate incentives. Indian status brings access to cheap land and, for more than a quarter of a century, inexpensive but superior housing. It means the availability of low-cost health care, which is improving in quality, and tribal employment programs. Finally, it has facilitated access to educational programs, like Head Start, which not only babysit the children of working mothers but may improve children's performance in elementary school, if only by ensuring that the children become fluent English speakers.

There are also constraints and incentives in being Graham County residents and "average Americans" that contribute to traditionalism and adaptiveness. The average Graham County resident, like the "typical American," is white; fullblood Cherokee Indians do not appear white. To a degree, however, a status as typical Graham County residents can be achieved, and once achieved, there are constraints on the type of behavior associated with the status. To be accepted completely in this Bible Belt area of the southern Appalachians, one must choose to be a fundamentalist Protestant Christian. Ultimately, most Snowbird individuals join one of the Indian community's churches, and an event like the Trail of Tears Singing emphasizes the community's Christianity. Sharing a trait as basic as religion emphasizes the community's commonality with local white communities and may allow more adaptability in other spheres.

The incentives associated with a status as Graham County residents are in some ways similar to those involved in an Indian status. As a Graham County resident, a Snowbird person has access to a public school education, county-sponsored employment programs, and the county's political power structure. To tap these resources fully, Snowbird people must be adaptive enough that in some situations other Graham County residents recognize them first as neighbors and county residents and only secondarily as Indians.

The next questions that must be asked are what roles Snowbird individuals choose to play, how these roles are acted out, and ultimately how those choices affect ethnic identity. In the council controversy where the stakes were especially high, role choices had more importance than in ordinary circumstances. The council controversy was thus a "transactual situation" in Barth's sense, and the choices made by Snowbird operated toward resolving the value dilemma of whether to act more Indian or white.[10] Behind the scenes, many Snowbird individuals appeared to act rather non-Indian, as when they consulted an attorney before the critical council session or privately explained to some councilmembers the motives of an individual hostile to Snowbird's cause. In the public arena, however, Snowbird individuals maximized their Indian identity, most notably when fluent English-speakers chose to speak in the Cherokee language. In other words, representatives of the Snowbird community engaged in what Goffman terms impression management.[11] The individuals from Snowbird over-communicated their real Indianness while under-communicating any non-Indian behavior. If enough Snowbird individuals find themselves in positions where it is advantageous to be real Indians, as in the council controversy, real Indianness will continue to be formalized and increasingly institutionalized in ceremonies like Snowbird's Trail of Tears Singing or the Eastern Band's Fall Festival.

Barth describes transactual situations, such as the council controversy, as: "the process which results where parties in the course of their interactions systematically try to assure that the value gained for them is greater or equal to the value lost. . . . It is meaningless to say that something has value unless people in real life seek it, prefer it to something of less value, in other words maximize value. This can only be true if they usually act strategically with respect to it."[12]

In the council controversy, Snowbird people chose the strategic argument that the 1889 Cherokee Charter and its 1897 amendment recognized only the Snowbird community as being part of the Cheoah Township, no reference being made to the Tomotla community. Quite simply, Snowbird, as a real Indian community, was claiming to have a contract with a group of Indians, the Eastern Band, which Tomotla did not have because it was not a real Indian community. That contract outlined the rights which were to flow from the Eastern Band to the Indian Township of Cheoah.

The council controversy also demonstrated how much Snowbird people value real Indianness in itself, not merely as a logically chosen strategy with which to confront the controversy. Barth explains that: "Values are empirical facts which may be discovered. . . . They are views about significance, worthwhileness, preferences in/for things and actions."[13] Snowbird people consciously want to preserve their identity as a real Indian community and to gain respect for that identity. People value fullbloodedness and talk about wanting their children to marry other Indians. They also value the Cherokee language. They worry lest it disappear, try to teach it to their children in the home, request that it be taught in the schools, talk about wanting their children to marry others who speak the Cherokee language, and joke that it is an American language while English is foreign. In households where only one parent speaks the language, that individual may frequently leave the children in the households of other relatives, usually the children's grandparents, where the language is used in the home. The express purpose for doing this is so the Cherokee language will be preserved.

The importance of the Cherokee language as a signal for Snowbird's ethnic identity as a real Indian community cannot be overemphasized. At present the number of Cherokee-language speakers in the United States is increasing, mostly among Oklahoma communities where Cherokee fullbloods have a much higher birth rate than white Indians. With approximately eleven thousand speakers, the Cherokee language "ranks seventh in number of speakers among American languages north of Mexico."[14] There are 127 Indian languages still spoken in the United States alone.[15] A Cherokee Bilingual Educational Program, based in Tahlequah, Oklahoma, demonstrates the importance of the Cherokee language. Among the Eastern Cherokees, linguist Duane King estimates that only 700 speakers reside on the populous Qualla Boundary while nearly everyone in the approximately 350-person Snowbird community speaks the language.[16] So, while Snowbird Cherokees are only about 5 percent of Eastern Cherokees, they are nearly one-third of all Cherokee language speakers in the east. He also notes a significant difference between speakers of the language who reside on the Qualla Boundary and those living in Snowbird: "The Snowbird Community has been unaffected by extensive tourism and has a balance of speakers in all age groups. Most of the fluent speakers on the Qualla Boundary, however, are past middle age."[17] In other words, the Cherokee language is in immediate danger of dying out on the Qualla Boundary, which has a higher percentage of white Indians who do not speak the language. By contrast, most people in Snowbird still speak the language fluently. In Snowbird, as on the Qualla Boundary, there are efforts to teach it in the schools. In Snowbird, however, most young adults speak the language because they were taught it in their homes as they grew up. There are even significant numbers of Snowbird children who speak the language. The Cherokee language could, it must be admitted, die out in a community as small as Snowbird, especially if intermarriage with non-speakers continues, but if the language survives anywhere in the east, it will survive in Snowbird. The Snowbird community thus functions as the keeper of a major part of Eastern Cherokee heritage in a situation where the delicate balance between traditionalism and acculturation could forever tip away from traditionalism.

The community is also quite conscious of maintaining a land base for a homeland, symbolized in the name of the Trail of Tears ceremony. The homeland signal was more tangibly evoked when the Indian Claims Commission awarded the Eastern Band nearly two million dollars for lands permanently lost to non-Indians. When this happened, Snowbird people talked of buying more reservation land. In fact, when the issue of the Claims money was presented before Tribal Council in 1972 (just before the 1973 council controversy), the only councilmembers who voted in favor of using the money to buy more reservation land and for other communal uses were the two Snowbird councilmembers. Every other councilmember voted for a per capita distribution of the money to individual Band members.

Snowbird people realize that tangible benefits can flow from status as Indians. During the council controversy they listed obvious advantages when they worried that losing the Cheoah council seats might mean losing a variety of economic advantages: for example, health care, employment opportunities, low-cost housing, and the Head Start School.

Like Gluckman, Barth suggests that: "Nobody sits down and speculates on the relative value of [something] . . . until this is a real dilemma of imminent choice."[18] The council controversy was a dramatic display of how the Snowbird community values its ethnic identity as a group of real Indians. With increasing involvement with Graham County whites and opportunities that flow from that involvement, Snowbird has been emphasizing other identities besides its real Indian identity. During the controversy over two seats in Tribal Council, however, Snowbird emphasized with renewed dedication its real Indian identity. Individuals from Snowbird, who on other occasions had not hesitated to address Tribal Council in English, switched almost exclusively to the Cherokee language at the session when the controversy was debated, despite the fact that many councilmembers hearing the case did not speak Cherokee, or if they did, they did not speak Snowbird's Atali dialect.

The Eastern Band of Cherokee Indians is a corporate group, legally a corporation under North Carolina laws. Barth suggests that individuals do not choose to belong to and mobilize corporate groups unless gains through membership are greater than losses.[19] For Snowbird people, Band membership means adhering to an Indian status, and it is as Indians and Band members that they receive the greatest advantages: housing, health care, claims money, bingo profits, education, and some employment. Even the Graham County Public Schools, which Snowbird students attend, might not have been so willing to integrate if federal BIA money did not flow into the school for each Indian child enrolled. Unlike white Indians, Snowbird people cannot gain full access to white communities by claiming status as whites. Thus, for fullbloods, there are not only incentives to Indian status but also constraints that ultimately prohibit the complete achievement of any other status.

The ultimate question to be answered concerns the persistence of an Indian ethnic identity, particularly as it revolves around the concept of "real Indianness," among the Eastern Cherokees. Barth asserts that ethnic groups can persist despite contact with the outside world, culture change, mobility, continuing relations with other groups of people, acceptance by other groups, and the osmosis of personnel across ethnic boundaries. If all of these things have happened to a group (and they have all occurred for the Eastern Cherokees), how has the group continued to exist as a distinct entity? The answer is found not only in making an inventory of the group's cultural content but by focusing on ethnic boundary maintenance.[20]

Depending upon the constraints and incentives involved, individual people largely choose whether or not to continue to live within the boundaries of an ethnic group, after having weighed the advantages of group membership. If enough people choose not to continue to live within the boundaries of an ethnic group, the group can cease to exist. If enough people choose to remain within the group's boundaries because the advantages to group membership prevail, the ethnic group persists. Social processes of exclusion, such as minimal-blood-degree requirements, set the boundaries which dictate what kinds of individuals may choose to be part of the group. In most of the world, an ethnic ascription is as basic to an individual's identity as sex and age "in that it constrains the incumbent in all his activities, not only in some defined social situations." As a status, ethnic identity is frequently superordinate to other statuses and is an individual's most fundamental type of identity.[21]

The individuals who choose to be part of a particular ethnic group do not necessarily have to be significantly culturally different from individuals in other ethnic groups in order for the groups to exist as identifiable social entities. Only certain cultural features need be maintained, "those which the actors themselves regard as significant," namely those cultural elements that serve as emblems or signals of ethnic boundaries. Both Barth and Spicer list language among frequently chosen signals. Barth goes on to list dress, house-form, and general style of life, and Spicer also includes homelands, music, dances, and heroes. People often ignore cultural differences, and "in some relationships radical differences are played down and denied."[22] The major signals chosen by traditionalist Cherokees belonging to the Snowbird community include the Cherokee language; the preservation of the special status of reservation land; the Trail of Tears Singing, which symbolizes the homeland represented in the reservation; native crafts; music sung in the Cherokee language; the occasional use of Indian dress and food; and native medicine. Also important, under Barth's category of general style of life, is the concept of both physical and cultural fullbloodedness.

Beyond such overt cultural signals, however, Barth emphasizes a second cultural dimension to the maintenance of ethnic identities, one he terms basic value orientations: "Since belonging to an ethnic category implies being a certain kind of person, having that basic identity, it also implies a claim to be judged, and to judge oneself, by those standards that are relevant to that identity." As with more overt signals, the main value orientations of an ethnic group do not necessarily encompass all of the cultural dimensions that can be applied to the group. Such values "may pervade all social life, or they may be relevant only in limited sectors of activity."[23] If many of these values "pervade all social life," as with traditionalist Cherokees, then they function not only as signals for ethnic boundaries but as a major part of the group's cultural content. Barth's concept certainly applies to traditionalist Cherokees who subscribe to the value orientation which Kupferer terms the Harmony Ethic.[24]

Many symbols chosen by groups to maintain ethnic boundaries are drawn from the highly visible material culture, as among Snowbird Cherokees: native crafts, dress, jewelry, food, and medicine. Some symbols are manifested quite overtly by certain patterns of behavior: the Cherokee language, music, and ceremonies. Other symbols ultimately have their bases in individuals' minds as concepts, beliefs, emotions, attitudes, and values, such as the Harmony Ethic. It is, however, the ideas in people's minds that serve as the blueprints for material culture and social interactions. In fact, such ethnic symbols can be found in all the places culture itself is found: within human beings themselves, their public behavior, and their artifacts. Since the symbols for ethnic boundary maintenance are drawn from once whole aboriginal cultures, it should not be surprising that they are drawn from all three sectors of culture: ideology, social organization, and technology. These aboriginal cultural signals alone, however, do not constitute complete cultural systems; acculturation has taken place. For the Snowbird Cherokees, however, one signal also makes up a significant aspect of the group's cultural content, the community's basic value orientation.

In the case of the Eastern Cherokees, Kupferer and Gulick have both described conservative Cherokee behavior as distinctively different from the behavior of local whites or more acculturated Cherokees.[25] Kupferer suggests that such traditionalist Cherokee behavior derives from a basically different value orientation, the Harmony Ethic, which also exists among the cultural conservatives of many other Native American groups across the United States.[26] Its basic features, as Kupferer describes them, are non-aggressiveness and non-competitiveness, particularly if the goal of aggressiveness is individual success. The use of intermediaries or neutral third parties is important in minimizing face-to-face hostility in interpersonal relations. Generosity is another important characteristic, and it occurs even when people cannot afford to be generous. A concept of immanent justice relieves people from feelings of needing to control others through direct interference. Finally, Kupferer makes this point about traditionalists and the Harmony Ethic: "Conservatives are sure of their identity as Indians . . . [as] a separate order of people."[27]

The Snowbird community does not subscribe consistently to the Harmony Ethic in all situations, and Barth suggests there is no reason to expect such uniformity of behavior. Snowbird people prefer Harmony Ethic behavior, especially an emphasis on non-aggressiveness and the superiority of group interests to individual concerns, so much so that when assertive behavior does occur, it is usually as a means of accomplishing some important group concern. Therefore, the Harmony Ethic does represent what Barth terms a basic value orientation and makes the Snowbird Cherokee individual "a certain kind of person."[28]

Cultures do change, and this is true even for the most culturally traditional individuals within a group. It should not be surprising that even as traditionalists become more successful at adapting to the world outside their ethnic group, they still remain traditionalists. The traditionalists in a group are the core of individuals around which ethnic identity is maintained. What is important is the persistence of a clear dichotomy between insiders, focusing on the core individuals, and outsiders, not the often changing culture of the insiders: "The critical focus of investigation . . . becomes the ethnic *boundary* that defines the group, not the cultural stuff that it encloses."[29] In the case of traditionalist Cherokees like the Snowbird people, the ethnic boundary is composed of a chain of signals including language, homeland, music, crafts, ceremonies, clothing, medicinal practices, food, a concept of physical and cultural fullbloodedness, and a value orientation based on harmony.

Crucial to analyzing ethnic group persistence are the rules controlling interethnic encounters and the role constraints under which individuals operate. Deviance from an expected type of behavior (in the case of the Cherokees, behavior deviating from the Harmony Ethic) will be sanctioned as inappropriate for members of a particular ethnic group. Certain spheres of activity are reserved exclusively for insiders, thus insulating whole segments of the culture from outsiders. With Snowbird people most of what goes on in families, the churches, and the community club is intended only for the members of the community, and attending outsiders, at least those who are not also traditionalist Cherokees, are effectively excluded through the use of a very important signal, the Cherokee language. There are, of course, other sectors of articulation where members of one ethnic group actively seek interaction with other people, such as most employment.

The Eastern Cherokees would not have persisted as a distinct ethnic group if there were not fundamental economic and environmental advantages to maintaining such a status. Barth suggests that ethnic relations can be analyzed from a perspective derived from an ecological model. He offers several variations on this model for the analysis of interethnic adaptations, and one of these seems to apply to the Cherokees. One of his hypothetical cases includes situations "where two or more interspersed groups are in fact in at least partial competition within the same niche. With time one would expect one such group to displace the other or an accommodation involving an increasing complementariness and interdependence to develop."[30]

In the Cherokees' case, in the early nineteenth century, especially in the fertile hill country of northern Georgia, Indians and whites were certainly in "competition within the same niche," and one group, the whites, did "displace the other," or most of them, by forcibly removing them.

Cherokees residing on the poorest lands, the nucleus of the Eastern Band, managed to avoid displacement. Practically every Native American group that remains within the southeast today has endured and been tolerated because it resides on lands of marginal value, such as swamps or mountains. But, as the population in the southern Appalachians grew, pressure for Cherokee land again saw Indians and whites in "competition within the same niche." Anticipating an allotment of Indian lands as private property (resulting from the Dawes Act of 1887), whites claiming minimal-Cherokee-blood degree moved onto the reservation lands of the Eastern Band displacing fullbloods from the better bottomlands. In the latter case, no one was displaced from the entire area, and what resulted was accommodation and assimilation, of a sort. The uneasy interdependence between real Indians and white Indians among the Eastern Cherokees dates from this era. Without the presence of the fullbloods, today the Eastern Band would have a difficult time legitimizing the group's Indianness.

Today it is white Indians (rather than whites) and real Indians who compete within the same niche. Reservation status to Cherokee lands effectively eliminates whites from the most important spheres of competition with fullbloods. And in the Cheoah Township fullbloods fought the last major battle to resist the competition with white Indians. Snowbird and Tomotla now compete within the same political niche. This most recent event in a long history of events has further eroded the culture and position of traditionalist Cherokees.

In the accommodation that resulted between the Eastern Band as a whole and neighboring whites, Indians largely ended up with the poorer lands.[31] The marginal nature of most Cherokee land has probably been responsible for the physical and ethnic survival of the Cherokees in the east. One of the major problems today is that the Eastern Cherokee population is growing (about nine thousand are enrolled now), but the group's land base is not expanding. This condition has been responsible for ever-increasing land disputes, despite the desire for harmony. Even access to poor, overcrowded land is important, however, because access to reservation land means direct access to high quality, low-cost housing, land for growing vegetable gardens, areas of unrestricted hunting and fishing, and, indirectly, other advantages like inexpensive health care, claims money, bingo profits, and employment opportunities. Ultimately, reservation lands are preserved, not through any "complementary accommodation" with local whites, but because the federal government legitimizes the reservation status of the land and sanctions its restriction to Eastern Cherokees (a policy endangered for all Native Americans during the federal government's termination decades, from 1954 to 1974). This condition encourages both fullbloods and white Indians to maintain their Band membership.

According to Barth, one of the most important characteristics about ethnic group persistence is that: "A drastic reduction of cultural difference between ethnic groups does not correlate in any simple way with a reduction in the organizational relevance of ethnic identities, or a breakdown in boundary-maintaining processes. . . . Cultural matter . . . can vary, be learnt, and change without any critical relation to the boundary maintenance of the ethnic group."[32]

As the cultures of ethnic groups change, members find that they can choose from among several basic strategies. Some individuals, such as some of the Cherokees labeled white Indians, may attempt to pass as members of the dominant society and become part of the osmosis of personnel across ethnic boundaries. In other cases, whole groups may assimilate culturally but not socially, to the point of achieving a minority group status, which sometimes seems to be the goal of the Bureau of Indian Affairs. Finally, the group may choose to emphasize their ethnic identity, particularly as do real Indians among the Cherokees: "using it to develop new positions and patterns to organize activities in those sectors formerly not found in their society, or inadequately developed for the new purposes."[33]

Ethnicity movements often have either political or religious overtones, or both, and if one looks beyond the Eastern Cherokee example to the continent-wide (even hemisphere-wide) resurgence of Native American identity, that movement seems to have such a dual nature.[34] Religious ceremonies, including events like the Trail of Tears Singing, have become vehicles by which Indians proclaim their fullbloodedness, whether physical or cultural. (The revival and perpetuation of the Sun Dance among many Indians of the Plains and the Potlatch among many Indians of the Northwest Coast are other examples.) Political battles, such as Snowbird's council controversy, often result in factional disputes between the so-called real members of the ethnic group and the pretenders to group membership (who are viewed as ultimately loyal to something outside the group) as often as they are directed against true outsiders.

By looking beyond the descriptions of Cherokee culture and analyses of culture change, it is possible to avoid the problems inherent in creating static behavioral typologies for the acculturating Eastern Cherokees. Instead, it is possible to analyze the process by which Eastern Cherokees adapt to the outside world while maintaining a distinct identity as Indians.

The concluding words of a program conducted at the Fall Festival by another group of Indians seem appropriate for a community like Snowbird: "We welcome the new world of harmony." Aboriginal Cherokee culture of the eighteenth century may be mourned by some scholars of the Cherokees, but to at least one community of Indians the essence of that culture survives today as signals for a Cherokee identity.

A close look at the Snowbird Cherokees of the 1990s reveals the dimensions of that new world of harmony. It is a society in which adaptation and tradition go hand in hand. Nowhere is that more obvious than in the generation of young adults in their twenties and thirties who are actively involved both in raising families and leading the community. Four young women immediately come to mind. Women have always had power and influence in Cherokee society, and these four are no exception. The three who are married are all wed to white men. They are therefore highly conscious of what strategies must be implemented to preserve Cherokee traditions in the next generation.

Shirley Jackson Oswalt, Ed and Ella Jackson's daughter, is an active member of Little Snowbird Baptist Church, along with her husband Mack and their children. Shirley Oswalt spends a lot of time at the new community store arranging for school supplies and other necessities to be available inexpensively to Snowbird children. When I think of a store not run for profit, I am reminded of Shirley's mother, Ella Jackson, who gave me a house for a year, rent-free. Shirley also plays a key role in the Junaluska Society whose goals are to perpetuate Cherokee history and to buy the property on which Junaluska is buried so that his bones are returned to Cherokee control, to the Cherokee homeland. Her uncle, Ned Long, meanwhile is involved in a lawsuit in Georgia to protect ancient Indian burials.

Shirley's older sister is Lou Ellen Jackson Jones. Lou and her husband Jerry will see the older of their two sons begin college with the financial assistance of the Ed Jackson Memorial Scholarship Fund, named for her father. Lou Jones and other Snowbird residents have worked for years to build the principle to a point where enough interest is yielded to provide two annual scholarships of a few hundred dollars each. Through local support as well as friends in other states, they still work to build the fund. While first preference is given to Indians, non-Indians may also receive support, and as Bud Jones leaves for college with his scholarship, so too will a white Graham County girl, thanks to Snowbird Indians.

Shirley and Lou's cousin is Patricia Long Holland who, with her husband Tommy and their sons, has an Indian business based on Tommy's abilities as a maker of custom cabinets. When the Qualla Housing Authority contracts to build new homes, they bid, usually successfully, to build and install the kitchen cabinets in houses in Snowbird, Tomotla, and the Qualla Boundary. Pat is within weeks of finishing her training to become a nurse like Lou Jones before her. Whether she will be able to join Lou at the Snowbird Health Clinic is uncertain, and she may have to continue to commute to an Asheville area hospital, a more than one-hundred-mile trip each way.

Brenda Long is Pat's younger sister. A college graduate, Brenda took a job at the local furniture plant like her two college-educated brothers. Areas of employment are limited in Graham County, and Brenda sees the value of her college education as more than merely a requirement for money or jobs. In 1990 Brenda lost her job for trying to unionize the factory. Interested workers also lost their jobs, and Brenda was locked in a room and intimidated by factory bosses. Her response has been to pursue the matter through the state's labor board and the courts. She points out she is in a position to do this for the good of the group since she still lives with her parents and does not have the financial burdens of a married person with children.

In these four women, and hundreds of other men and women in the

Snowbird community, one can see traditionalist Indian behavior on a daily basis, particularly a concern with the good of the group beyond one's immediate family, whether it involves education, health, employment, or any of a number of areas. Snowbird may beat the odds. The decline in the number of Cherokee-language speakers may be stabilized. Shirley Oswalt, a fluent speaker who has recently learned to read and write in the Cherokee syllabary, will soon begin to teach that skill to two of her nephews. But even if the language continues to decline, the Harmony Ethic is thriving. Brenda Long, whose mother, Shirley Long, is white, does not speak Cherokee, and yet she wonders how some people can see families suffering because of low wages and not feel an obligation to help others. She may not "talk Indian," but she surely "acts Indian."

A program presented at the tribal-operated Museum of the Cherokee Indian, which opened on June 15, 1976, talks about ethnic persistence in yet another way: "Like the mountains and streams around us, the Cherokee people and Cherokee heritage will endure for ages to come." The old world of harmony may be gone forever, but the new world of harmony persists.

Notes

INTRODUCTION

1. Gilliam Jackson, "Cultural Identity for the Modern Cherokees," *Appalachian Journal* 2 (1975): 282.

2. John Gulick, *Cherokees at the Crossroads* (Chapel Hill: Institute for Research in Social Science, University of North Carolina, 1973), p. 125.

3. Ibid., p. 126.

4. Ibid., p. 17.

5. John R. Finger, *The Eastern Band of Cherokees: 1819–1900* (Knoxville: University of Tennessee Press, 1984), p. 9.

ONE. LAND OF THE SKY PEOPLE

1. Traveller Bird (Tsisghwanai), *The Path to Snowbird Mountain: Cherokee Legends* (New York: Farrar, Straus and Giroux, 1972), p. 4.

2. James Mooney, *Myths of the Cherokee*, Bureau of American Ethnology, nineteenth annual report (Washington, D.C.: Smithsonian Institution, 1900); Leonard Bloom, "The Acculturation of the Eastern Cherokee" (Ph.D. diss., Duke University, 1937); William Harlan Gilbert, Jr., *The Eastern Cherokee*, Bureau of American Ethnology, bulletin 133 (Washington, D.C.: U.S. Government Printing Office, 1943); John Gulick, *Cherokees at the Crossroads* (Chapel Hill: Institute for Research in Social Science, University of North Carolina, 1973); Harriet Jane Kupferer, *The "Principal People," 1960: A Study of Cultural and Social Groups of the Eastern Cherokee*, Bureau of American Ethnology, bulletin 196, no. 78 (Washington, D.C.: U.S. Government Printing Office, 1966); Laurence French, "Emerging Social Problems Among the Qualla Cherokee," *Appalachian Notes* 3 (1975): 17–23.

3. Gulick, *Crossroads*, p. 17; Duane H. King, "A Grammar and Dictionary of the Cherokee Language" (Ph.D. diss., University of Georgia, 1975).

4. Rodney L. Leftwich, *Arts and Crafts of the Cherokee* (Cullowhee, N.C.: Land of the Sky Press, 1970); Raymond D. Fogelson and Paul Kutsche, "Cherokee Economic Cooperatives: The Gadugi," in *Symposium on Cherokee and Iroquois Culture,* ed. William N. Fenton and John Gulick, Bureau of American Ethnology, bulletin 180, no. 11 (Washington, D.C.: U.S. Government Printing Office, 1961); Max E. White, "Contemporary Usage of Native Plant Foods by the Eastern Cherokees," *Appalachian Journal* 2 (1975): 323–26.

5. Gaston Litton, "Enrollment Records of the Eastern Band of Cherokee Indians," *North Carolina Historical Review* 17 (July 1940): 207.

6. Henry Thompson Malone, *Cherokees of the Old South* (Athens: University of Georgia Press, 1956), pp. 107–9; John R. Finger, *The Eastern Band of Cherokees, 1819–1900* (Knoxville: University of Tennessee Press, 1984), pp. 13–14.

7. Douglas C. Wilms, "Cherokee Slave Ownership Prior to the Removal" (Paper presented at the Symposium on New Directions in Cherokee Studies, ninth annual meeting of the Southern Anthropological Society, Blacksburg, Virginia, 1974).

8. Finger, *Eastern Band,* p. 9; Mooney, *Myths,* p. 113; Henry M. Owl, "The Eastern Band of Cherokee Indians Before and After the Removal" (master's thesis, University of North Carolina, Chapel Hill, 1929), p. 101.

9. Marion Starkey, *The Cherokee Nation* (New York: Knopf, 1946), pp. 27–28.

10. Litton, "Enrollment," pp. 207–8.

11. Brewton Berry, *Almost White* (New York: Macmillan, 1963); Gilbert, *Eastern Cherokee,* p. 438; Edward T. Price, "A Geographic Analysis of White-Indian-Negro Racial Mixtures in the Eastern United States," *Annals of the Association of American Geographers* 43 (1953): 149.

12. Gulick, *Crossroads,* p. 19.

13. Mooney, *Myths,* p. 163.

14. Finger, *Eastern Band,* p. 163.

15. Mattie Russel, "William Holland Thomas: White Chief of the North Carolina Cherokees" (Ph.D. diss., Duke University, 1956), p. 46.

16. Mary Young, "Cherokee Removal: A Case Study in Federal Policy" (Paper presented at the second annual meeting of the Symposium on the American Indian, Northeastern State College, Tahlequah, Oklahoma, 1974), p. 12.

17. Margaret Walker Freel, *Our Heritage: The People of Cherokee County, North Carolina, 1540–1955* (Asheville, N.C.: Miller, 1956), p. 400.

18. *Cherokee Progress and Challenge* (Cherokee, N.C.: Eastern Band of Cherokee Indians, 1972), p. 8.

19. Finger, *Eastern Band.*

20. "Quallatown Indians," *Friends' Weekly Intelligencer* 6 (1849): 2–3.

21. Ibid., p. 2.

22. Charles Lanman, *Letters from the Alleghany Mountains* (New York: Putnam, 1849), p. 95.

23. *Cherokee Progress*, p. 8.

24. Finger, *Eastern Band*, p. 29.

25. Ibid., pp. 107–8; Kupferer, "*Principal People*," pp. 229–30.

26. Finger, *Eastern Band*, p. 114.

27. Anna Gritts Kilpatrick and Jack F. Kilpatrick, eds. and trans., *The Shadow of Sequoyah: Social Documents of the Cherokees, 1862–1964* (Norman: University of Oklahoma Press, 1965), p. 8.

28. *Cherokee Progress*, p. 8.

29. Russel, "White Chief," p. 427.

30. *Cherokee Progress*, p. 8.

31. Russel, "White Chief," p. 431.

32. Kupferer, "*Principal People*," p. 232.

33. Eastern Cherokee Bureau of Indian Affairs Superintendent, Letter, in *Annual Report of the Commissioner of Indian Affairs* (East Point, Ga: Federal Regional Records Center, 1931).

34. Gulick, *Crossroads*, pp. 20–21.

35. Litton, "Enrollment," p. 222.

36. Mooney, *Myths*, p. 176.

37. Owl, "Cherokee Indians," p. 142.

38. Litton, "Enrollment," p. 231.

39. Ibid., p. 216.

40. Wilbur G. Zeigler and Ben S. Grosscup, *The Heart of the Alleghanies, or Western North Carolina* (Raleigh, N.C.: Alfred Williams, 1883), pp. 36–37.

41. Lanman, *Letters*, p. 95.

42. Ibid., pp. 96–99.

43. Litton, "Enrollment," p. 216.

44. Eastern Cherokee BIA Superintendent, *Annual Report*, 1931.

45. Ibid.

46. Litton, "Enrollment," p. 216.

47. Gulick, *Crossroads*, p. 22; *Cherokee Progress*, p. 39.

48. Gulick, *Crossroads*, pp. 18–19; *Cherokee Progress*, p. 39.

49. Eastern Cherokee BIA Superintendent, Letter, in *Annual Report of the Commissioner of Indian Affairs* (East Point, Ga.: Federal Regional Records Center, 1958).

50. *Cherokee Progress*, pp. 33–35.

51. Leftwich, *Arts and Crafts*, p. 61.

52. *Cherokee Progress,* p. 47.
53. "Nostalgia Isn't What It Used to Be," *Cherokee One Feather* 5, no. 39 (1972): 3.
54. Fogelson and Kutsche, "The Gadugi."
55. Kupferer, *"Principal People,"* pp. 290–95.

TWO. "REAL INDIANS"

1. James Mooney, *Myths of the Cherokee,* Bureau of American Ethnology, nineteenth annual report (Washington, D.C.: Smithsonian Institution, 1900); William Harlan Gilbert, Jr., *The Eastern Cherokee,* Bureau of American Ethnology, bulletin 133 (Washington, D.C.: U.S. Government Printing Office, 1943); Leonard Bloom, "The Acculturation of the Eastern Cherokee" (Ph.D. diss., Duke University, 1937); John Gulick, *Cherokees at the Crossroads,* rev. ed. (Chapel Hill: Institute for Research in Social Science, University of North Carolina, 1973); Harriet Jane Kupferer, *The "Principal People," 1960: A Study of Cultural and Social Groups of the Eastern Cherokee,* Bureau of American Ethnology, bulletin 196, no. 78 (Washington, D.C.: U.S. Government Printing Office, 1966).
2. Fredrik Barth, ed., *Ethnic Groups and Boundaries: The Social Organization of Culture Difference* (Boston: Little, Brown, 1969), pp. 9, 21.
3. Ibid., p. 10.
4. Vine Deloria, Jr., *Custer Died for Your Sins: An Indian Manifesto* (New York: Avon, 1969), pp. 170–71.
5. Gulick, *Crossroads,* p. 7.
6. Harald Eidheim, "The Lappish Movement: An Innovative Political Process," in *Local-Level Politics,* ed. Marc J. Swartz (Chicago: Aldine, 1968); Anthony F. C. Wallace, "Revitalization Movements: Some Theoretical Considerations," *American Anthropologist* 58 (1956): 264–81; John J. Honigmann, "Intercultural Relations at Great Whale River," *American Anthropologist* 54 (1954): 510–22.
7. Barth, *Ethnic Groups.*
8. Edward H. Spicer, "Persistent Cultural Systems: A Comparative Study of Identity Systems That Can Adapt to Contrasting Environments," *Science* 174 (1971): 795–800.
9. Deloria, *Custer Died,* p. 230.
10. Barth, *Ethnic Groups,* p. 17.
11. Kupferer, *"Principal People,"* pp. 289–311.
12. Steven Polgar, "Biculturation of Mesquakie Teenage Boys," *American Anthropologist* 62 (1960): 217–35.

13. Paul B. Horton and Chester L. Hunt, *Sociology* (New York: McGraw-Hill, 1976), pp. 354–55.

14. *Cherokee Progress and Challenge* (Cherokee, N.C.: Eastern Band of Cherokee Indians, 1972), p. 47.

15. Wayne Dennis, *Group Values Through Children's Drawings* (New York: John Wiley and Sons, 1966), pp. 2, 7.

16. Gilliam Jackson, "Cultural Identity for the Modern Cherokees," *Appalachian Journal* 2 (1975): 280.

17. Ibid.

18. Eidheim, "Lappish Movement," p. 207; Spicer, "Persistent Cultural Systems."

19. Mooney, *Myths*, pp. 250–52.

20. Raymond D. Fogelson, "Change, Persistence, and Accommodation in Cherokee Medico-Magical Beliefs," in *Symposium on Cherokee and Iroquois Culture*, ed. William N. Fenton and John Gulick, Bureau of American Ethnology, bulletin 180, no. 21 (Washington, D.C.: U.S. Government Printing Office, 1961), p. 218.

21. Ibid., p. 136.

22. Kupferer, *"Principal People,"* pp. 289–99.

23. Robert E. Daniels, "Cultural Identities Among the Oglala Sioux," in *The Modern Sioux: Social System and Reservation Culture*, ed. Ethel Nurge (Lincoln: University of Nebraska Press, 1970), p. 210.

24. Ibid., p. 229.

25. Murray L. Wax, *Indian Americans: Unity and Diversity* (Englewood Cliffs, N.J.: Prentice-Hall, 1971), p. 119.

26. Deloria, *Custer Died*, pp. 242–43.

27. Eleanor Burke Leacock and Nancy Oestreich Lurie, eds., *North American Indians in Historical Perspective* (New York: Random House, 1971), p. 12.

28. Jackson, "Cultural Identity," pp. 280, 283.

29. "Traditional Dances Taught in School," *Cherokee One Feather* 9, no. 6 (1976): 1, 3.

THREE. A POLITICAL CONTROVERSY

1. J. van Velsen, "The Extended-case Method and Situational Analysis," in *The Craft of Social Anthropology*, ed. A. L. Epstein (London: Social Science Paperbacks, 1967), p. 140.

2. Max Gluckman, *Analysis of a Social Situation in Modern Zululand*, Rhodes-Livingstone Papers, no. 28 (Manchester: Manchester University Press, 1958).

3. Fredrik Barth, *Models of Social Organization*, Royal Anthropological Institute Occasional Paper, no. 23 (Glasgow: University Press, 1966).

4. Fredrik Barth, ed., *Ethnic Groups and Boundaries: The Social Organization of Culture Difference* (Boston: Little, Brown, 1969).

5. John Gulick, *Cherokees at the Crossroads*, rev. ed. (Chapel Hill: Institute for Research in Social Science, University of North Carolina, 1973), p. 120.

6. Ibid., p. 6.

7. *Cherokee Progress and Challenge* (Cherokee, N.C.: Eastern Band of Cherokee Indians, 1972), p. 4.

8. Harriet Jane Kupferer, *The "Principal People," 1960: A Study of Cultural and Social Groups of the Eastern Cherokee*, Bureau of American Ethnology, bulletin 196, no. 78 (Washington, D.C.: U.S. Government Printing Office, 1966), p. 232.

9. Murray L. Wax, *Indian Americans: Unity and Diversity* (Englewood Cliffs, N.J.: Prentice-Hall, 1971), p. 119.

10. "Six Candidates in Race for Vice Chief of E.B.C.I." *Cherokee One Feather*, August 29, 1973, 1.

11. "Tribe to Elect Vice Chief, 14 Councilmen Thursday, Sept. 6," *Cherokee One Feather*, September 5, 1973, 1.

12. "Tribal Judges Record Large Election Turnout," *Cherokee One Feather*, September 12, 1973, 1.

13. "200 Additional Homes Approved for Qualla Housing Authority," *Cherokee One Feather*, January 29, 1975, 1.

14. "$73,600 Grant for Building," *Cherokee One Feather* 8, no. 18 (1976): 1.

15. *Cherokee Progress*, p. 47.

16. "200 Additional Homes," p. 1.

17. "Enrollment Notice," *Cherokee One Feather* 7, no. 5 (1974): 1.

18. "Council Summary," *Cherokee One Feather*, August 14, 1974, 1–2.

19. Laurence French, "Emerging Social Problems Among the Qualla Cherokee," *Appalachian Notes* 3 (1975): 17–23.

20. Duane Harold King, "A Grammar and Dictionary of the Cherokee Language" (Ph.D. diss., University of Georgia, 1975).

21. Charles H. Holzinger, "Some Observations on the Persistence of Aboriginal Cherokee Personality Traits," in *Symposium on Cherokee and Iroquois Culture*, ed. William N. Fenton and John Gulick, Bureau of American Ethnology, bulletin 180, no. 22 (Washington, D.C.: U.S. Government Printing Office, 1961), pp. 234–35.

22. French, "Emerging Social Problems," p. 20.

23. Gulick, *Crossroads*, p. 120.

24. *Cherokee Progress*, p. 64.

25. Ibid., p. 63.

26. Ibid., p. 64.

27. Ibid., p. 11.

28. Vine Deloria, Jr., *Custer Died for Your Sins: An Indian Manifesto* (New York: Avon, 1969), pp. 240–42, 245.

29. Barth, *Ethnic Groups*, p. 15.

30. Gulick, *Crossroads*, p. 19.

31. Ibid., p. 20.

32. French, "Emerging Social Problems," p. 20.

FOUR. A CEREMONY

1. Robert E. Daniels, "Cultural Identities Among the Oglala Sioux," in *The Modern Sioux: Social System and Reservation Culture,* ed. Ethel Nurge (Lincoln: University of Nebraska Press, 1970), p. 233.

2. Fredrik Barth, *Models of Social Organization* (Glasgow: University Press, 1966), pp. 17–21.

3. Ibid., p. 18.

4. Daniels, "Cultural Identities," p. 232.

5. Ibid., p. 240.

FIVE. THE NEW WORLD OF HARMONY

1. J. van Velsen, "The Extended-case Method and Situational Analysis," in *The Craft of Social Anthropology,* ed. A. L. Epstein (London: Social Science Paperbacks, 1967), p. 134.

2. John Gulick, *Cherokees at the Crossroads,* rev. ed. (Chapel Hill: Institute for Research in Social Science, University of North Carolina, 1973), p. 17.

3. Robert E. Daniels, "Cultural Identities Among the Oglala Sioux," in *The Modern Sioux: Social System and Reservation Culture,* ed. Ethel Nurge (Lincoln: University of Nebraska Press, 1970), pp. 204–5.

4. Ibid., pp. 211–12.

5. van Velsen, "Extended-case Method," pp. 129, 136.

6. Fredrik Barth, *Models of Social Organization* (Glasgow: University Press, 1966), pp. 2, 12.

7. Edward H. Spicer, "Persistent Cultural Systems: A Comparative Study of Identity Systems That Can Adapt to Contrasting Environments," *Science* 174 (1971): 795–800.

8. Barth, *Models;* David Bidney, *Theoretical Anthropology* (New York: Columbia University Press, 1953); Leslie A. White, "The Concept of Culture," *American Anthropologist* 61 (1959): 227–51.

9. Barth, *Models*, p. 1.

10. Ibid.

11. Erving Goffman, *Strategic Interaction* (Philadelphia: University of Pennsylvania Press, 1969), p. 141.

12. Barth, *Models,* pp. 4–5.

13. Ibid., p. 12.

14. Duane Harold King, "A Grammar and Dictionary of the Cherokee Language" (Ph.D. diss., University of Georgia, 1975), p. 1.

15. William L. Leap, "Ethnics, Emics, and the New Ideology: The Identity Potential of Indian English," in *Social and Cultural Identity: Problems of Persistence and Change,* ed. Thomas K. Fitzgerald, Southern Anthropological Society Proceedings, no. 8 (Athens: University of Georgia Press, 1974), p. 54.

16. King, "Grammar," p. 2.

17. Ibid.

18. Barth, *Models,* p. 18; Max Gluckman, *Analysis of a Social Situation in Modern Zululand,* Rhodes-Livingstone Papers, no. 28 (Manchester: Manchester University Press, 1958), pp. 73–74.

19. Barth, *Models,* p. 24.

20. Fredrik Barth, ed., *Ethnic Groups and Boundaries: The Social Organization of Culture Difference* (Boston: Little, Brown, 1969), pp. 9–10, 21.

21. Ibid., pp. 17, 13.

22. Ibid., p. 14.

23. Ibid.

24. Harriet Jane Kupferer, *The "Principal People," 1960: A Study of Cultural and Social Groups of the Eastern Cherokee,* Bureau of American Ethnology, bulletin 196, no. 78 (Washington, D.C.: U.S. Government Printing Office, 1966).

25. Ibid.; Gulick, *Crossroads.*

26. Kupferer, *"Principal People,"* pp. 289–99; Nancy Oestreich Lurie, "The Contemporary American Indian Scene," in *North American Indians in Historical Perspective,* ed. Eleanor Burke Leacock and Nancy Oestreich Lurie (New York: Random House, 1971), pp. 444–48.

27. Kupferer, *"Principal People,"* pp. 290, 292–95, 298.

28. Barth, *Ethnic Groups,* p. 14.

29. Ibid., p. 15.

30. Ibid., pp. 19–20.

31. Gulick, *Crossroads,* p. 19.

32. Barth, *Ethnic Groups,* pp. 32–33, 38.

33. Ibid., p. 33.

34. Ibid., p. 34.

Bibliography

Anders, Gary Carson. "The Internal Colonization of Cherokee Native Americans." *Development and Change* 10 (1979): 41–55.

Barth, Fredrik. *Models of Social Organization*. Royal Anthropological Institute Occasional Paper, no. 23. Glasgow: University Press, 1966.

——. "Analytical Dimensions in the Comparison of Social Organizations." *American Anthropologist* 74 (1972): 207–20.

——, ed. *Ethnic Groups and Boundaries: The Social Organization of Culture Difference*. Boston: Little, Brown, 1969.

Berry, Brewton. *Almost White*. New York: Macmillan, 1963.

Bidney, David. *Theoretical Anthropology*. New York: Columbia University Press, 1953.

Bird, Traveller (Tsisghwanai). *The Path to Snowbird Mountain: Cherokee Legends*. New York: Farrar, Straus and Giroux, 1972.

Bloom (Broom), Leonard. "The Acculturation of the Eastern Cherokee." Ph.D. diss., Duke University, 1937.

——. "The Cherokee Clan: A Study in Acculturation." *American Anthropologist* 41 (1939): 266–68.

——. "The Acculturation of the Eastern Cherokee: Historical Aspects." *North Carolina Historical Review* 19 (1942): 323–58.

Cherokee Progress and Challenge. Cherokee, N.C.: Eastern Band of Cherokee Indians, 1972.

Clifton, James A. "Factional Conflict and the Indian Community: The Prairie Potawatomi Case." In *The American Indian Today*, edited by Stuart Levine and Nancy Oestreich Lurie, 115–32. Deland, Fla.: Everett Edwards, 1968.

Coe, Joffre L. "Cherokee Archeology." In *Symposium on Cherokee and Iroquois Culture*, edited by William N. Fenton and John Gulick, 51–60. Bureau of American Ethnology, bulletin 180, no. 7. Washington, D.C.: U.S. Government Printing Office, 1961.

Daniels, Robert E. "Cultural Identities Among the Oglala Sioux." In *The Modern Sioux: Social System and Reservation Culture*, edited by Ethel Nurge, 198–245. Lincoln: University of Nebraska Press, 1970.

Deloria, Vine, Jr. *Custer Died for Your Sins: An Indian Manifesto.* New York: Avon, 1969.

Dennis, Wayne. *Group Values Through Children's Drawings.* New York: John Wiley and Sons, 1966.

Dickens, Roy S., Jr. *Cherokee Prehistory: The Pisgah Phase in the Appalachian Summit Region.* Knoxville: University of Tennessee Press, 1976.

Eastern Cherokee Bureau of Indian Affairs (BIA) Superintendent. Letter. In *Annual Report of the Commissioner of Indian Affairs.* East Point, Ga.: Federal Regional Records Center, 1931.

———. Letter. In *Annual Report of the Commissioner of Indian Affairs.* East Point, Ga.: Federal Regional Records Center, 1958.

Ehle, John. *Trail of Tears: The Rise and Fall of the Cherokee Nation.* New York: Anchor Press, 1988.

Eidheim, Harald. "The Lappish Movement: An Innovative Political Process." In *Local-Level Politics*, edited by Marc J. Swartz, 205–16. Chicago: Aldine, 1968.

Fenton, William N., and John Gulick, eds. *Symposium on Cherokee and Iroquois Culture.* Bureau of American Ethnology, bulletin 180. Washington, D.C.: U.S. Government Printing Office, 1961.

Finger, John R. *The Eastern Band of Cherokees, 1819–1900.* Knoxville: University of Tennessee Press, 1984.

Fogelson, Raymond D. "Change, Persistence, and Accommodation in Cherokee Medico-Magical Beliefs." In *Symposium on Cherokee and Iroquois Culture*, edited by William N. Fenton and John Gulick, 213–25. Bureau of American Ethnology, bulletin 180, no. 21. Washington, D.C.: U.S. Government Printing Office, 1961.

Fogelson, Raymond D., and Paul Kutsche. "Cherokee Economic Cooperatives: The Gadugi." In *Symposium on Cherokee and Iroquois Culture*, edited by William N. Fenton and John Gulick, 83–123. Bureau of American Ethnology, bulletin 180, no. 11. Washington, D.C.: U. S. Government Printing Office, 1961.

Freel, Margaret Walker. *Our Heritage: The People of Cherokee County, North Carolina, 1540–1955.* Asheville, N.C.: Miller, 1956.

French, Laurence. "Emerging Social Problems Among the Qualla Cherokee." *Appalachian Notes* 3 (1975): 17–23.

French, Laurence, and Jim Hornbuckle. "An Analysis of Indian Violence: The Cherokee Example." *American Indian Quarterly* 3 (1977): 335–56.

———, eds. *The Cherokee Perspective.* Boone, N.C.: Appalachian Consortium Press, 1981.

Frizzell, George E. *The Legal Status of the Eastern Band of Cherokee Indians.* Master's thesis. Western Carolina University, Cullowhee, 1981.

Gearing, Frederick O. "The Structural Poses of 18th-Century Cherokee Villages." *American Anthropologist* 60 (1958): 1148–57.

Gilbert, William Harlan, Jr. *The Eastern Cherokee.* Bureau of American Ethnology, bulletin 133. Washington, D.C.: U.S. Government Printing Office, 1943.

Gluckman, Max. *Analysis of a Social Situation in Modern Zululand.* Rhodes-Livingstone Papers, no. 28. Manchester: Manchester University Press, 1958.

Goffman, Erving. *Strategic Interaction.* Philadelphia: University of Pennsylvania Press, 1969.

Goodwin, Gary C. *Cherokees in Transition: A Study of Changing Culture and Environment Prior to 1775.* Chicago: University of Chicago Press, 1977.

Graham County Centennial: 1872–1972. Robbinsville, N.C.: Graham County Centennial 1972, Inc., 1972.

Gulick, John. *Cherokees at the Crossroads.* 1960. Rev. ed. Chapel Hill: Institute for Research in Social Science, University of North Carolina, 1973.

Holzinger, Charles H. "Some Observations on the Persistence of Aboriginal Cherokee Personality Traits." In *Symposium on Cherokee and Iroquois Culture,* edited by William N. Fenton and John Gulick, 227–37. Bureau of American Ethnology, bulletin 180, no. 22. Washington, D.C.: U.S. Government Printing Office, 1961.

Honigmann, John J. "Intercultural Relations at Great Whale River." *American Anthropologist* 54 (1954): 510–22.

Horton, Paul B., and Chester L. Hunt. *Sociology.* New York: McGraw-Hill, 1976.

Hudson, Charles M. *The Southeastern Indians.* Knoxville: University of Tennessee Press, 1976.

Jackson, Gilliam. "Cultural Identity for the Modern Cherokees." *Appalachian Journal* 2 (1975): 280–83.

Keel, Bennie C. *Cherokee Archaeology: A Study of the Appalachian Summit.* Knoxville: University of Tennessee Press, 1976.

Kilpatrick, Anna Gritts, and Jack F. Kilpatrick, eds. and trans. *The Shadow of Sequoyah: Social Documents of the Cherokees, 1862–1964.* Norman: University of Oklahoma Press, 1965.

———. *Chronicles of Wolfetown: Social Documents of the North Carolina Cherokees, 1850–1862.* Bureau of American Ethnology, bulletin 196, no. 80. Washington, D.C.: U.S. Government Printing Office, 1966.

King, Duane Harold. "A Grammar and Dictionary of the Cherokee Language." Ph.D. diss., University of Georgia, 1975.

King, Duane H., ed. *The Cherokee Indian Nation: A Troubled History.* Knoxville: University of Tennessee Press, 1979.

Kluckhohn, Clyde, and Dorothea Leighton. *The Navaho*. 1946. Rev. ed. Lucy H. Wales and Richard Kluckhohn, eds. Garden City, N.Y.: Natural History Library, Doubleday, 1962.

Kupferer, Harriet Jane. *The "Principal People," 1960: A Study of Cultural and Social Groups of the Eastern Cherokee*. Bureau of American Ethnology, bulletin 196, no. 78. Washington, D.C.: U.S. Government Printing Office, 1966.

———. "The Isolated Eastern Cherokee." In *The American Indian Today*, edited by Stuart Levine and Nancy Oestreich Lurie, 213–325. Deland, Fla.: Everett Edwards, 1968.

Lanman, Charles. *Letters from the Alleghany Mountains*. New York: Putnam, 1849.

Leacock, Eleanor Burke, and Nancy Oestreich Lurie, eds. *North American Indians in Historical Perspective*. New York: Random House, 1971.

Leap, William L. "Ethnics, Emics, and the New Ideology: The Identity Potential of Indian English." In *Social and Cultural Identity: Problems of Persistence and Change*, edited by Thomas K. Fitzgerald, 51–62. Southern Anthropological Society Proceedings, no. 8. Athens: University of Georgia Press, 1974.

Leftwich, Rodney L. *Arts and Crafts of the Cherokee*. Cullowhee, N.C.: Land of the Sky Press, 1970.

Lewis, Thomas M. N., and Madeline Kneberg. *Tribes That Slumber*. Knoxville: University of Tennessee Press, 1958.

Littlefield, Daniel F., Jr. *The Cherokee Freedmen: From Emancipation to American Citizenship*. Westport, Conn.: Greenwood Press, 1978.

Litton, Gaston. "Enrollment Records of the Eastern Band of Cherokee Indians." *North Carolina Historical Review* 17 (July 1940): 199–231.

Lurie, Nancy Oestreich. "The Contemporary American Indian Scene." In *North American Indians in Historical Perspective*, edited by Eleanor Burke Leacock and Nancy Oestreich Lurie, 418–80. New York: Random House, 1971.

McLoughlin, William G. *The Cherokee Ghost Dance and Other Essays*. Macon, Ga.: Mercer University Press, 1984.

———. *Cherokees and Missionaries, 1789–1839*. New Haven: Yale University Press, 1984.

McLoughlin, William G., and Walter H. Conser, Jr. "The Cherokees in Transition: A Statistical Analysis of the Federal Cherokee Census of 1835." *Journal of American History* 64 (1977): 678–703.

Malone, Henry Thompson. *Cherokees of the Old South*. Athens: University of Georgia Press, 1956.

Mitchell, J. Clyde. *The Kalela Dance: Aspects of Social Relationships Among Urban Africans in Northern Rhodesia*. Rhodes-Livingstone Papers, no. 27. Manchester: Manchester University Press, 1956.

Mooney, James. *Myths of the Cherokee*. Bureau of American Ethnology, nineteenth annual report. Washington, D.C.: U.S. Government Printing Office, 1900.

Moulton, Gary E. *John Ross, Cherokee Chief.* Athens: University of Georgia Press, 1978.

Neely, Sharlotte. "The Quaker Era of Cherokee Indian Education, 1880–1892." *Appalachian Journal* 2 (1975): 314–22.

———. "Acculturation and Persistence among North Carolina's Eastern Band of Cherokee Indians." In *Southeastern Indians since the Removal Era,* edited by Walter L. Williams, 154–73. Athens: University of Georgia Press, 1979.

———. "Forced Acculturation in the Eastern Cherokee Bureau of Indian Affairs Schools, 1892–1933." In *Contemporary Political Organizations of Native North America,* edited by Ernest L. Schuskey, 85–106. Washington, D.C.: University Press of America, 1979.

———. "Highway Construction Through Cherokee Lands: Cultural Impact Statement." Prepared for Cherokee Legal Services, Cherokee, North Carolina. Typescript, 1979.

———. Foreword to *The Cherokee Perspective,* edited by Laurence French and Jim Hornbuckle, iii–iv. Boone, N.C.: Appalachian Consortium Press, 1981.

———. "Snowbird Cherokees: Adaptation and Ethnic Preservation." In *Cultural Adaptation to Mountain Environments,* edited by Patricia D. Beaver and Burton L. Purrington, 107–21. Southern Anthropological Society Proceedings, no. 17. Athens: University of Georgia Press, 1984.

O'Donnell, James H., III. *Southern Indians in the American Revolution.* Knoxville: University of Tennessee Press, 1973.

Ortiz, Alfonso. *The Tewa World: Space, Time, Being, and Becoming in a Pueblo Society.* Chicago: University of Chicago Press, 1969.

Oswalt, Wendell H. *This Land Was Theirs: A Study of the North American Indian.* New York: John Wiley and Sons, 1978.

Owl, Henry M. "The Eastern Band of Cherokee Indians Before and After the Removal." Master's thesis, University of North Carolina, Chapel Hill, 1929.

Paredes, J. Anthony. "The Emergence of Contemporary Eastern Creek Indian Identity." In *Social and Cultural Identity: Problems of Persistence and Change,* edited by Thomas K. Fitzgerald, 63–80. Southern Anthropological Proceedings, no. 8. Athens: University of Georgia Press, 1974.

Perdue, Theda. "Rising from the Ashes: *The Cherokee Phoenix* as an Ethnohistorical Source." *Ethnohistory* 24 (1977): 207–18.

———. *Slavery and the Evolution of Cherokee Society, 1540–1866.* Knoxville: University of Tennessee Press, 1979.

Perry, Samuel D. "Religious Festivals in Cherokee Life." *Indian Historian* 12 (1979): 20–22, 28.

Polgar, Steven. "Biculturation of Mesquakie Teenage Boys." *American Anthropologist* 62 (1960): 217–35.

Pollitzer, William S., et al. "Blood Types of the Cherokee Indians." *American Journal of Physical Anthropology* 20 (1962): 33–43.

Price, Edward T. "A Geographic Analysis of White-Indian-Negro Racial Mixtures in the Eastern United States." *Annals of the Association of American Geographers* 43 (1953): 138–55.

Purrington, Burton L., ed. "New Perspectives on the Cherokees: Special Cherokee Issue." *Appalachian Journal* 2 (1975): 250–356.

"Quallatown Indians." *Friends' Weekly Intelligencer* 6 (1849): 2–3.

Redman, Susan M. "United States Indian Policy and the Eastern Cherokees, 1838–1889." Master's thesis, University of Cincinnati, 1980.

Russel, Mattie. "William Holland Thomas: White Chief of the North Carolina Cherokees." Ph.D. diss., Duke University, 1956.

Sharpe, Bill. *A New Geography of North Carolina.* Vol. 3. Raleigh, N.C.: Sharpe, 1961.

Speck, Frank G., and Leonard Broom (Bloom) with Will West Long. *Cherokee Dance and Drama.* Berkeley: University of California Press, 1951.

Speck, Frank G., and Claude E. Schaeffer. "The Mutual-aid Volunteer Company of the Eastern Cherokee." *Journal of the Washington Academy of Sciences* 35 (1945): 169–79.

Spicer, Edward H. "Persistent Cultural Systems: A Comparative Study of Identity Systems That Can Adapt to Contrasting Environments." *Science* 174 (1971): 795–800.

Starkey, Marion. *The Cherokee Nation.* New York: Knopf, 1946.

Swanton, John R. *Indians of the Southeastern United States.* Bureau of American Ethnology, bulletin 137. Washington, D.C.: U.S. Government Printing Office, 1946.

Thomas, Robert K. "Eastern Cherokee Acculturation." Typescript, 1958.

van Velsen, J. "The Extended-case Method and Situational Analysis." In *The Craft of Social Anthropology,* edited by A. L. Epstein, 129–49. London: Social Science Paperbacks, 1967.

Wallace, Anthony F. C. "Revitalization Movements: Some Theoretical Considerations." *American Anthropologist* 58 (1956): 264–81.

Wallace, Anthony F. C., with Sheila C. Steen. *The Death and Rebirth of the Seneca.* New York: Knopf, 1970.

Wax, Murray L. *Indian Americans: Unity and Diversity.* Englewood Cliffs, N.J.: Prentice-Hall, 1971.

Weeks, Charles J. "The Eastern Cherokee and the New Deal." *North Carolina Historical Review* 53 (1976): 303–19.

White, Leslie A. "The Concept of Culture." *American Anthropologist* 61 (1959): 227–51.

White, Max E. "Contemporary Usage of Native Plant Foods by the Eastern Cherokees." *Appalachian Journal* 2 (1975): 323–26.

Williams, Sharlotte Neely. "Epilogue: Cherokees at the Crossroads, 1973." In *Cherokees at the Crossroads*, by John Gulick, 175–94. Chapel Hill: Institute for Research in Social Science, University of North Carolina, 1973.

Wilms, Douglas C. "Cherokee Slave Ownership Prior to the Removal." Paper presented at the Symposium on New Directions in Cherokee Studies, ninth annual meeting of the Southern Anthropological Society, Blacksburg, Virginia, 1974.

Young, Mary. "Cherokee Removal: A Case Study in Federal Policy." Paper presented at the second annual meeting of the Symposium on the American Indian, Northeastern State College, Tahlequah, Oklahoma, 1974.

Zeigler, Wilbur G., and Ben S. Grosscup. *The Heart of the Alleghanies, or Western North Carolina*. Raleigh, N.C.: Alfred Williams, 1883.

Index

2